POEMS

1925–1940

POEMS

1925-1940

BY LOUIS MACNEICE

RANDOM HOUSE NEW YORK

POEMS

1925-1940

BY LOUIS MACNEICE

RANDOM HOUSE · NEW YORK

FIRST PRINTING

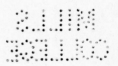

ACKNOWLEDGMENT

Some of these poems have previously appeared in the following English periodicals: *The New Statesman and Nation, The Spectator, The Criterion, The Times Literary Supplement, The London Mercury, Life and Letters, The Listener, Horizon, New Verse, New Writing* and in the following American periodicals: *The New Republic, The Nation, The Partisan Review, Common Sense, Poetry, The New Yorker, Furioso, Harper's Bazaar* and *The Kenyon Review.*

I also wish to acknowledge my indebtedness to Harcourt, Brace and Company, Inc., for permission to reprint excerpts from *Out of the Picture.*

CONTENTS

Out of the Picture: 1936–1937

Poems: 1936–1938

Autumn Journal: 1938

Poems: 1939–1940

FOREWORD

When a man collects his poems, people think he is dead. I am collecting mine not because I am dead, but because my past life is. Like most other people in the British Isles I have little idea what will happen next. I shall go on writing, but my writing will presumably be different.

Everything I have put into this book seems to me worth reading, though some of the poems, especially the softer adolescent ones in the first section, are very limited. I have included a little light verse because man's lightheadedness should sometimes be articulate.

All poems are not written the same way. Critics forget this. There are occasions for flatness and hyperbole, for concentration and diffuseness, for regular and irregular form, for both the unusual and the obvious, for uplift and understatement. A few of these poems are perhaps obscure, but others will only be found obscure by people who try to be too clever; my poem "Snow," for instance, means exactly what it says.

"Autumn Journal," the long topical poem I wrote in the Fall of 1938, is in a sense a failure; it fails in depth. I had foreseen that failure. We shall not be capable of depth—of tragedy or *great* poetry—until we have made sense of our world. "Autumn Journal" remains a journal —topical, personal, rambling, but, failing other things, honest.

I should like people to read these poems aloud; with a few exceptions each line has been approved by my ear. And I would ask my readers not to be snobs; I write poetry not because it is smart to be a poet but because I enjoy it, as one enjoys swimming or swearing, and also because it is my road to freedom and knowledge.

L. M.

October, 1940

I

EARLY POEMS: 1925–1929

TRAINS IN THE DISTANCE

Trains came threading quietly through my dozing child-
    hood,
Gentle murmurs nosing through a summer quietude,
Drawing in and out, in and out, their smoky ribbons,
Parting now and then, and launching full-rigged gal-
    leons
And scrolls of smoke that hung in a shifting epitaph.
Then distantly the noise declined like a descending
    graph,
Sliding downhill gently to the bottom of the distance
(For now all things are there that all were here once);
And so we hardly noticed when that metal murmur
    came
But it brought us assurance and comfort all the same,
And in the early night they soothed us to sleep,
And the chain of the rolling wheels bound us in deep
Till all was broken by that menace from the sea,
The steel-bosomed siren calling bitterly.

                                    [1926]

GLASS FALLING

The glass is going down. The sun
Is going down. The forecasts say
It will be warm, with frequent showers.
We ramble down the showery hours
And amble up and down the day.
Mary will wear her black goloshes
And splash the puddles on the town;

3

And soon on fleets of macintoshes
The rain is coming down, the frown
Is coming down of heaven showing
A wet night coming, the glass is going
Down, the sun is going down.

[1926]

THE CREDITOR

The quietude of a soft wind
Will not rescind
My debts to God, but gentle-skinned
His finger probes. I lull myself
In quiet in diet in riot in dreams,
In dopes in drams in drums in dreams
Till God retire and the door shut.
But
Now I am left in the fire-blaze
The peacefulness of the fire-blaze
Will not erase
My debts to God for His mind strays
Over and under and all ways
All days and always.

[1929]

KOSMOS

A million whirling spinning-wheels of flowing gossamer,
A million hammers jangling on the anvils of the sky,
The crisp chip of chisels and the murmuring of saws
And the flowing ripple of water from a million taps,

4

With the champ of griffin-horses with their heads in
    sacks of hay
And sawdust flitting to and fro in new-born fragrancy.
But not the same for all—flooding over weedy rocks,
A green sea singing like a dream, and on the shore
Fair round pebbles with eggy speckles half transparent,
And brown sodden tangles of odorous wrack.

[1925]

POUSSIN

In that Poussin the clouds are like golden tea,
And underneath the limbs flow rhythmically,
The cupids' blue feathers beat musically,
And we dally and dip our spoon in the golden tea.
The tea flows down the steps and up again,
An old-world fountain, pouring from sculptured lips,
And the chilly marble drop like sugar slips
And is lost in the dark gold depths, and the refrain
Of tea-leaves floats about and in and out,
And the motion is still as when one walks and the moon
Walks parallel but relations remain the same.
And thus we never reach the dregs of the cup,
Though we drink it up and drink it up and drink it up,
And thus we dally and dip our spoon.

[1926]

5

EVENING INDOORS

In this evening room there is no stir, no fuss;
The silken shade of the oil-light is diaphanous,
And so come other noises through the noise of the clock
Transparent as the shade, as a girl's frock.
There is no crease, no fold ruffling the room at all;
The glass fringe of the shade seems a summer waterfall,
Like August insects purring over mown grass
The flames blend and pass, incend and end and pass.
Like the calm blue marriage of the sky and sea,
Or a blue-veiled Madonna beaming vacancy,
See that Madonna snuff out the shaded light
And stroke with soothing hand asleep the night.

[1927]

HAPPY FAMILIES

The room is all a stupid quietness,
Cajoled only by the fire's caress;
We loll severally about and sit
Severally and do our business severally,
For there's a little bit for everybody;
But that's not all there is to it.

Crusted in sandstone, while the wooden clock
Places two doctor fingers on his mouth,
We seem fossils in rock,
Or leaves turned mummies in drouth,
And garnered into a mouldy shrubbery corner
Where the wind has done with us. When we are old
The gardener will use us for leaf-mould.

6

Dutifully sitting on chair, lying on sofa,
Standing on hearth-rug, here we are again,
John caught the bus, Joshua caught the train,
And I took a taxi, so we all got somewhere;
No one deserted, no one was a loafer,
Nobody disgraced us, luckily for us
No one put his foot in it or missed the bus.

But the wind is a beggar and always
Raps at front door, back door, side door;
In spite of the neat placard that says
"NO HAWKERS HERE" he knocks the more,
He blows loose paper into petulance
And ruffles the brazier's fiery hair; and once
He caught me suddenly surreptitiously
And heft me out of my shell. We'll pass that over
And forget about it and quietly sit
Knitting close, sitting close under cover.

Snuff out the candle, for the cap, I think,
Seems to fit, excellently fit.
Te saluto—in a fraction, half a wink—
But that's not all there is to it.

                                        [1928]

PERIPETEIA

Descending out of the grey
Clouds elephant trunk
Twitches away
Hat;

THAT
Was *not* what I expected,
A
Misdirected
Joke it seemed to me;
"What about a levitation?" I had said,
Preening head for halo,
All alert, combed, sanctified,
I thank Thee, Lord, I am not like other men
WHEN
Descending out of the grey
Clouds elephant trunk . . .

[and so *ad nauseam.*]
[1929]

THE COURT HISTORIAN

Under the coffered gilt the court historian
Turns the mothy silks that time has left him;
His beard waves in the dark, and the shades about him
Thrust their delicate hands and twitch his elbow,
Begging remembrance. It is touch and go
For half a paragraph of immortality—
To be, not to be, sink or swim.
Sternly he fronts the frittered waves that gather
Round his cold mind with the beacon light upon it,
Spreading bitter wisdom on the water.
He squats and stitches in his corner; he records
Mutinies, rapes, and blackguardly robberies,
Births, deaths, burials of the lower classes,
Births, deaths, funerals of the upper classes;

8

He bites the thread of their lives that death already
Snapt so thoroughly. But the court historian
Understudies death, but more becomingly.
Come here a minute and watch him through the lattice;
You said he was alone, did you not?
Then I wonder who that is who is looking over
His shoulder at his manuscript; which says,
'All the great ministers and their mistresses are gone:
So and so died on the twenty-first of January;
So and so was assassinated; and so and so
Passed away in a fit on Saturday evening. . . .'
But on his shoulder a finger taps and says,
'So much for them, but what about the court historian?'

[1927]

A CLASSICAL EDUCATION

The well-oiled heckling Greeks have left their anchors
To rust on the pier-head among the pushing groundsel,
And the Romans too have gone at the goose step
Under a crooked arch into silence.
Why, then, do I loiter round these chartered sanctuaries,
Holding the basin to gowned and spectacled Pilates
While they suffer these ghosts to be martyred over and
    over?
Will no one shake a rattle at these crows,
Or take a little trowel and carefully cover
The painted skulls? And yet one might suppose
On a windy night their teeth were chattering
In frivolous phalæcians or stern hexameters;

9

Or, groping among the mortuary porticoes,
Might hear a heart mark time, or possibly find
A poet like a pale candle guttering
On a worn window-sill in the wind.

[1928]

SAILOR'S FUNERAL

The deep ways of man are doped now and dead and gone,
Under sea there rings for his obsequies a carillon,
Slow the sable hooves exalt and sway and halt anon,
They have found the sailor's bones in the sea; drowned
     and gone.

Shove a coffin over them, and with grey clay it cover,
They use his bones for dumb-bells beneath the cliffs of
     Dover.
More sailors come to shore, one like another,
And who will mind at all now, if one's passed over?

Now he weds the sea-weed, where never any sun shone,
And bells knell his wedding, with a red dead carillon,
Tolling for his soul, prisoned in the water wan,
Shed his red beauty, his bright life dead and gone.

[1926]

RIVER IN SPATE

The river falls and over the walls the coffins of cold
    funerals
Slide deep and sleep there in the close tomb of the pool,
And yellow waters lave the grave and pebbles pave its
    mortuary,
And the river horses vault and plunge with their assault
    and battery,
And helter-skelter the coffins come and the drums beat
    and the waters flow,
And the panther horses lift their hooves and paw and
    shift and draw the bier,
The corpses blink in the rush of the river, and out of the
    water their chins they tip
And quaff the gush and lip the draught and crook their
    heads and crow,
Drowned and drunk with the cataract that carries them
    and buries them
And silts them over and covers them and lilts and
    chuckles over their bones;
The organ-tones that the winds raise will never pierce
    the water ways,
So all they will hear is the fall of hooves and the distant
    shake of harness,
And the beat of the bells on the horses' heads and the
    undertaker's laughter,
And the murmur that will lose its strength and blur at
    length to quietness,
And afterwards the minute heard descending, never
    ending heard,
And then the minute after and the minute after the min-
    ute after.   [1927]

11

CANDLE POEM

I have no clock, yet I can hear
The minutes pass while I sit here
Tired but free from tedium
And mark the waning cylinder.

To-morrow will be another day,
And to-day will then be yesterday,
To click the bonds of business
From Saturday to Saturday.

Another night will follow, but
My candle will then be a candle butt
And the door that is day and day's division
Will have opened once and shut.

Close your armoured books and mark
The waning cylinder that drips
Fluid time from pallid lips,
Making an island in the dark.

This island is too small, I fear;
Dark horses fret away the shore,
And I can build no breakwater
But only close a desperate ear
And mark the waning cylinder.

[1927]

12

TRAPEZE

Beyond the dykes of cloud and steel spikes of air
The sun's breathing golden prickling fur
Over a vibrant belly warned us
Leap the beast will sometime
Breaking every bridge of the well-worn thoroughfare
Of the zodiac. Gone the fawning yawning purr
Changed for a foam-flash. Gone the indolent industry
That padded round the treadmill, raised the crops
And helped to work the tides. Look up and see
Fiery now . . . how he angrily
Flicks his tongue hungry around his chops.

Blood slavers over the evening sky;
Bees are at compline, not knowing that soon
An end is set to respectability.
On the skyline shaggy spears of grass
Itch ominously and the moon
Limps on a crutch whose ferrule taps to us
Doom (if rightly we decodify).

Still we are happy even if our nerves
Twitch now and again as the grasses do.
We know that we only live on sufferance
And that however well this star-seat serves
Our purpose as trapezists for this once,
In any case the rope is wearing through.
Tom Tom Terry, Tom Tom Terry.
The glutton tit swings in the cocoanut
In the equinoctial gale.
This circus-job means death sooner or later

13

From wild beasts or fire among the tinsel.
Tom Tom Terry, Tom Tom Terry.

[1929]

SPRING SUNSHINE

In a between world, a world of amber,
The old cat on the sand-warm window-sill
Sleeps on the verge of nullity.

Spring sunshine has a quality
Transcending rooks and the hammering
Of those who hang new pictures,
Asking if it is worth it
To clamour and caw, to add stick to stick for ever.

If it is worth while really
To colonise any more the already populous
Tree of knowledge, to portion and reportion
Bits of broken knowledge brittle and dead,
Whether it would not be better
To hide one's head in the warm sand of sleep
And be embalmed without hustle or bother.

The rooks bicker heckle bargain always
And market carts lumber—
Let me in the calm of the all-humouring sun
Also indulge my humour
And bury myself beyond creaks and cawings
In a below world, a bottom world of amber.

[1929]

CRADLE SONG FOR MIRIAM

The clock's untiring fingers wind the wool of darkness
And we all lie alone, having long outgrown our cradles
(Sleep, sleep, Miriam)
And the flames like faded ladies always unheeded simper
And all is troubledness.

Soft the wool, dark the wool
Is gathered slowly, wholly up
Into a ball, all of it.

And yet in the back of the mind, lulled all else,
There is Something unsleeping, un-tamperable-with,
Something that whines and scampers
And like the ladies in the grate will not sleep nor forget
    itself,
Clawing at the wool like a kitten.

Sleep, sleep, Miriam,
And as for this animal of yours
He must be cradled also,
That he may not unravel this handiwork of forgetfulness,
That he may not philander with the flames before they
    die.

The world like a cradle rises and falls
On a wave of confetti and funerals
And sordor and stinks and stupid faces
And the deity making bored grimaces.

Oh, what a muddle he has made of the wool
(God will to-morrow have his hands full),
You must muzzle your beast, you must fasten him
For the whole of life—the interim.

Through the interim we pass
Everyone under an alias
Till they gather the strands of us together
And wind us up for ever and ever.

The clock's fingers wind, wind the wool of Lethe,
(Sleep, sleep, Miriam)
It glides across the floor drawn by hidden fingers
And the beast droops his head
And the fire droops its flounces
And winks a final ogle out of the fading embers
But no one pays attention;

This is too much, the flames say, insulted,
We who were once the world's beauties and now
No one pays attention
No one remembers us.

[1928]

MAYFLY

Barometer of my moods to-day, mayfly,
Up and down one among a million, one
The same at best as the rest of the jigging mayflies,
One only day of May alive beneath the sun.

The yokels tilt their pewters and the foam
Flowers in the sun beside the jewelled water.
Daughter of the South, call the sunbeams home
To nest between your breasts. The kingcups
Ephemeral are gay gulps of laughter.

Gulp of yellow merriment; cackle of ripples;
Lips of the river that pout and whisper round the reeds.
The mayfly flirting and posturing over the water
Goes up and down in the lift so many times for fun.

'When we are grown up we are sure to alter
Much for the better, to adopt solider creeds;
The kingcup will cease proffering his cup
And the foam will have blown from the beer and the
    heat no longer dance
And the lift lose fascination and the May
Change her tune to June—but the trouble with us may-
    flies
Is that we never have the chance to be grown up.'

They never have the chance, but what of time they have
They stretch out taut and thin and ringing clear;
So we, whose strand of life is not much more,
Let us too make our time elastic and
Inconsequently dance above the dazzling wave.

Nor put too much on the sympathy of things,
The dregs of drink, the dried cups of flowers,
The pathetic fallacy of the passing hours
When it is we who pass them—hours of stone
Long rows of granite sphinxes looking on.

It is we who pass them, we the circus masters
Who make the mayflies dance, the lapwings lift their
    crests,
The show will soon shut down, its gay-rags gone,
But when this summer is over let us die together,
I want always to be near your breasts.

[1929]

II

POEMS: 1931–1935

BELFAST

The hard cold fire of the northerner
Frozen into his blood from the fire in his basalt
Glares from behind the mica of his eyes
And the salt carrion water brings him wealth.

Down there at the end of the melancholy lough
Against the lurid sky over the stained water
Where hammers clang murderously on the girders
Like crucifixes the gantries stand.

And in the marble stores rubber gloves like polyps
Cluster, celluloid, painted ware, glaring
Metal patents, parchment lampshades, harsh
Attempts at buyable beauty.

In the porch of the chapel before the garish Virgin
A shawled factory-woman as if shipwrecked there
Lies a bunch of limbs glimpsed in the cave of gloom
By us who walk in the street so buoyantly and glib.

Over which country of cowled and haunted faces
The sun goes down with a banging of Orange drums
While the male kind murders each its woman
To whose prayer for oblivion answers no Madonna.
                                                [1931]

BIRMINGHAM

Smoke from the train-gulf hid by hoardings blunders
 upward, the brakes of cars
Pipe as the policeman pivoting round raises his flat hand,
 bars
With his figure of a monolith Pharaoh the queue of
 fidgety machines
(Chromium dogs on the bonnet, faces behind the triplex
 screens),
Behind him the streets run away between the proud
 glass of shops,
Cubical scent-bottles artificial legs arctic foxes and elec-
 tric mops,
But beyond this centre the slumward vista thins like a
 diagram:
There, unvisited, are Vulcan's forges who doesn't care a
 tinker's damn.
Splayed outwards through the suburbs houses, houses
 for rest
Seducingly rigged by the builder, half-timbered houses
 with lips pressed
So tightly and eyes staring at the traffic through bleary
 haws
And only a six-inch grip of the racing earth in their con-
 crete claws;
In these houses men as in a dream pursue the Platonic
 Forms
With wireless and cairn terriers and gadgets approximat-
 ing to the fickle norms
And endeavour to find God and score one over the neigh-
 bour

By climbing tentatively upward on jerry-built beauty
    and sweated labour.
The lunch hour: the shops empty, shopgirls' faces relax
Diaphanous as green glass, empty as old almanacs
As incoherent with ticketed gewgaws tiered behind their
    heads
As the Burne-Jones windows in St. Philip's broken by
    crawling leads;
Insipid colour, patches of emotion, Saturday thrills
(This theatre is sprayed with 'June')—the gutter take our
    old playbills,
Next week-end it is likely in the heart's funfair we shall
    pull
Strong enough on the handle to get back our money; or
    at any rate it is possible.
On shining lines the trams like vast sarcophagi move
Into the sky, plum after sunset, merging to duck's egg,
    barred with mauve
Zeppelin clouds, and Pentecost-like the cars' headlights
    bud
Out from sideroads and the traffic signals, crème de
    menthe or bull's blood,
Tell one to stop, the engine gently breathing, or to go on
To where like black pipes of organs in the frayed and
    fading zone
Of the West the factory chimneys on sullen sentry will
    all night wait
To call, in the harsh morning, sleep-stupid faces through
    the daily gate.

[1933]

TURF-STACKS

Among these turf-stacks graze no iron horses
Such as stalk, such as champ in towns and the soul of
    crowds,
Here is no mass-production of neat thoughts
No canvas shrouds for the mind nor any black hearses:
The peasant shambles on his boots like hooves
Without thinking at all or wanting to run in grooves.

But those who lack the peasant's conspirators,
The tawny mountain, the unregarded buttress,
Will feel the need of a fortress against ideas and against
    the
Shuddering insidious shock of the theory-vendors,
The little sardine men crammed in a monster toy
Who tilt their aggregate beast against our crumbling
    Troy.

For we are obsolete who like the lesser things
Who play in corners with looking-glasses and beads;
It is better we should go quickly, go into Asia
Or any other tunnel where the world recedes,
Or turn blind wantons like the gulls who scream
And rip the edge off any ideal or dream.

                                  [1932]

UPON THIS BEACH

Upon this beach the falling wall of the sea
Explodes its drunken marble
Amid gulls' gaiety.

Which ever-crumbling masonry, cancelling sum,
No one by any device can represent
In any medium.

Turn therefore inland, tripper, foot on the sea-holly,
Forget those waves' monstrous fatuity
And boarding bus be jolly.

[1932]

CIRCE

'. . . *vitreamque Circen*'

Something of glass about her, of dead water,
Chills and holds us,
Far more fatal than painted flesh or the lodestone of live
    hair
This despair of crystal brilliance.
Narcissus' error
Enfolds and kills us—
Dazed with gazing on that unfertile beauty
Which is our own heart's thought.
Fled away to the beasts
One cannot stop thinking; Timon
Kept on finding gold.

25

In parrot-ridden forest or barren coast
A more importunate voice than bird or wave
Escutcheoned on the air with ice letters
Seeks and, of course, finds us
(Of course, being our echo).

Be brave, my ego, look into your glass
And realise that that never-to-be-touched
Vision is your mistress.   *[1931]*

SPRING VOICES

The small householder now comes out warily
Afraid of the barrage of sun that shouts cheerily,
Spring is massing forces, birds wink in air,
The battlemented chestnuts volley green fire,
The pigeons banking on the wind, the hoots of cars,
Stir him to run wild, gamble on horses, buy cigars;
Joy lies before him to be ladled and lapped from his
     hand—
Only that behind him, in the shade of his villa, memories
     stand
Breathing on his neck and muttering that all this has hap-
     pened before,
Keep the wind out, cast no clout, try no unwarranted
     jaunts untried before,
But let the spring slide by nor think to board its car
For it rides West to where the tangles of scrap-iron are;
Do not walk, these voices say, between the bucking
     clouds alone
Or you may loiter into a suddenly howling crater, or fall,
     jerked back, garrotted by the sun.   *[1933]*

26

MUSEUMS

Museums offer us, running from among the buses,
A centrally heated refuge, parquet floors and sarcopha-
  guses,
Into whose tall fake porches we hurry without a sound
Like a beetle under a brick that lies, useless, on the
  ground.
Warmed and cajoled by the silence the cowed cypher
  revives,
Mirrors himself in the cases of pots, paces himself by
  marble lives,
Makes believe it was he that was the glory that was Rome,
Soft on his cheek the nimbus of other people's martyr-
  dom,
And then returns to the street, his mind an arena where
  sprawls
Any number of consumptive Keatses and dying Gauls.

[1933]

CONTACT

The trains pass and the trains pass, chains of lighted win-
  dows,
A register in an unknown language
For these are the trains in which one never goes.

The familiar rhythm but the unknown implications
Delight like a dead language
Which never shocks us by banal revelations.

So listening for the night express coming down the way
I receive the expected whistle of the engine
Sharp and straight on the ear like stigmata.

[1933]

NATURE MORTE

(*Even so it is not so easy to be dead*)

As those who are not athletic at breakfast day by day
Employ and enjoy the sinews of others vicariously,
Shielded by the upheld journal from their dream-punc-
    turing wives
And finding in the printed word a multiplication of their
    lives,
So we whose senses give us things misfelt and misheard
Turn also, for our adjustment, to the pretentious word
Which stabilises the light on the sun-fondled trees
And, by photographing our ghosts, claims to put us at
    our ease;
Yet even so, no matter how solid and staid we contrive
Our reconstructions, even a still life is alive
And in your Chardin the appalling unrest of the soul
Exudes from the dried fish and the brown jug and the
    bowl.

[1933]

TO A COMMUNIST

Your thoughts make shape like snow; in one night only
The gawky earth grows breasts,
Snow's unity engrosses
Particular pettiness of stones and grasses.
But before you proclaim the millennium, my dear,
Consult the barometer—
This poise is perfect but maintained
For one day only.   *[1933]*

EGO

We with our Fair pitched among the feathery clover
Are always cowardly and never sober,
Drunk with steam-organs, thigh-rub and cream-soda
—We cannot remember enemies in this valley.

As chestnut candles turn to conkers, so we
Knock our brains together extravagantly
Instead of planting them to make more trees
—Who have not as yet sampled God's malice.

But to us urchins playing with paint and filth
A prophet scanning the road on the hither hills
Might utter the old warning of the old sin
—Avenging youth threatening an old war.

Crawling down like lava or termites
Nothing seduces, nothing dissolves, nothing affrights
You who scale off masks and smash the purple lights
—But I will escape, with my dog, on the far side of the
    Fair.   *[1933]*

SUNDAY MORNING

Down the road some one is practising scales,
The notes like little fishes vanish with a wink of tails,
Man's heart expands to tinker with his car
For this is Sunday morning, Fate's great bazaar;
Regard these means as ends, concentrate on this Now,
And you may grow to music or drive beyond Hindhead
    anyhow,
Take corners on two wheels until you go so fast
That you can clutch a fringe or two of the windy past,
That you can abstract this day and make it to the week
    of time
A small eternity, a sonnet self-contained in rhyme.

But listen, up the road, something gulps, the church spire
Opens its eight bells out, skulls' mouths which will not
    tire
To tell how there is no music or movement that ensures
Escape from the weekday time. Which deadens and
    endures.

[1933]

AUGUST

The shutter of time darkening ceaselessly
Has whisked away the foam of may and elder
And I realise how now, as every year before,
Once again the gay months have eluded me.

For the mind, by nature stagey, welds its frame
Tomb-like around each little world of a day;
We jump from picture to picture and cannot follow
The living curve that is breathlessly the same.

While the lawn-mower sings moving up and down
Spirting its little fountain of vivid green,
I, like Poussin, make a still-bound fête of us
Suspending every noise, of insect or machine.

Garlands at a set angle that do not slip,
Theatrically (and as if for ever) grace
You and me and the stone god in the garden
And Time who also is shown with a stone face.

But all this is a dilettante's lie,
Time's face is not stone nor still his wings,
Our mind, being dead, wishes to have time die
For we being ghosts cannot catch hold of things.

[1933]

THE GLACIER

Just as those who gaze get higher than those who climb
A paradox unfolds on any who can tamper with time.
Where bus encumbers upon bus and fills its slot
Speed up the traffic in a quick motion film of thought
Till bus succeeds bus so identically sliding through
That you cannot catch the fraction of a chink between
     the two;
But they all go so fast, bus after bus, day after day,
Year after year, that you cannot mark any headway,
But the whole stream of traffic seems to crawl
Carrying its dead boulders down a glacier wall
And we who have always been haunted by the fear of
     becoming stone
Cannot bear to watch that catafalque creep down
And therefore turn away to seemingly slower things
And rejoice there to have found the speed of fins and
     wings
In the minnow-twistings of the latinist who alone
Nibbles and darts through the shallows of the lexicon
Or among the plate-glass cases in sombre rooms where
Eyes appraise the glazen life of majolica ware
Or where a gardener with trowel and rheumatic pains
Pumps up the roaring sap of vegetables through their
     veins.

[1933]

PERSEUS

Borrowed wings on his ankles,
Carrying a stone death,
The hero entered the hall,
All in the hall looked up,
Their breath frozen on them,
And there was no more shuffle or clatter in the hall at all.

So a friend of a man comes in
And leaves a book he is lending or flowers
And goes again, alive but as good as dead,
And you are left alive, no better than dead,
And you dare not turn the leaden pages of the book or
    touch the flowers, the hooded and arrested hours.

Close your eyes,
There are suns beneath your lids,
Or look in the looking-glass in the end room—
You will find it full of eyes,
The ancient smiles of men cut out with scissors and kept
    in mirrors.

Ever to meet me comes, in sun or dull,
The gay hero swinging the Gorgon's head
And I am left, with the dull drumming of the sun, sus-
    pended and dead,
Or the dumb grey-brown of the day is a leper's cloth,
And one feels the earth going round and round the globe
    of the blackening mantle, a mad moth.

[1934]

APRIL

Our April must replenish the delightful wells,
Bucket's lip dipping, light on the sleeping cells,
Man from his vigil in the wintry chapel
Will card his skin with accurate strigil.
O frivolous and astringent spring
We never come full circle, never remember
Self behind self years without number,
A series of dwindling mirrors, but take a tangent line
And start again. Our April must replenish
Our bank-account of vanity and give our doors a coat
    of varnish.
Leave the tedium of audits and of finding correct
For the gaiety of places where people collect
For the paper rosettes of the stadium and the plaudits.
And you, let you paint your face and sleek your leg with
    silk
Which is your right to do
As gay trams run on tracks and cows give milk.
Sharp sun-strop, surface-gloss, and momentary caprice
These are what we cherish
Caring not if the bridges and the embankments
Of past and future perish and cease;
Before the leaves grow heavy and the good days vanish
Hold out your glasses which our April must replenish.
                           [1934]

MORNING SUN

Shuttles of trains going north, going south, drawing
    threads of blue,
The shining of the lines of trams like swords,
Thousands of posters asserting a monopoly of the good,
    the beautiful, the true,
Crowds of people all in the vocative, you and you,
The haze of the morning shot with words.

Yellow sun comes white off the wet streets but bright
Chromium yellows in the gay sun's light,
Filleted sun streaks the purple mist,
Everything is kissed and reticulated with sun
Scooped-up and cupped in the open fronts of shops
And bouncing on the traffic that never stops.

And the street fountain blown across the square
Rainbow-trellises the air and sunlight blazons
The red butcher's and scrolls of fish on marble slabs,
Whistled bars of music crossing silver sprays
And horns of cars, touché, touché, rapiers' retort, a mov-
    ing cage,
A turning page of shine and sound, the day's maze.

But when the sun goes out, the streets go cold, the hang-
    ing meat
And tiers of fish are colourless and merely dead,
And the hoots of cars neurotically repeat and the tiptoed
    feet
Of women hurry and falter whose faces are dead;
And I see in the air but not belonging there

The blown grey powder of the fountain grey as the ash
That forming on a cigarette covers the red.

[1935]

CUCKOO

Cuckoo across the poppies
        Making myth—
Simeon on his pillar
        Stands in the air alone.

Without context
        Not looking down,
Personification
        Of distance.

Nothing to be seen
        But a stone posture,
The shape of the song
        Of the cuckoo.

[1935]

TRAIN TO DUBLIN

Our half-thought thoughts divide in sifted wisps
Against the basic facts repatterned without pause,
I can no more gather my mind up in my fist
Than the shadow of the smoke of this train upon the
        grass—
This is the way that animals' lives pass.

The train's rhythm never relents, the telephone posts
Go striding backwards like the legs of time to where
In a Georgian house you turn at the carpet's edge
Turning a sentence while, outside my window here,
The smoke makes broken queries in the air.

The train keeps moving and the rain holds off,
I count the buttons on the seat, I hear a shell
Held hollow to the ear, the mere
Reiteration of integers, the bell
That tolls and tolls, the monotony of fear.

At times we are doctrinaire, at times we are frivolous,
Plastering over the cracks, a gesture making good,
But the strength of us does not come out of us.
It is we, I think, are the idols and it is God
Has set us up as men who are painted wood,

And the trains carry us about. But not consistently so,
For during a tiny portion of our lives we are not in trains,
The idol living for a moment, not muscle-bound
But walking freely through the slanting rain,
Its ankles wet, its grimace relaxed again.

All over the world people are toasting the King,
Red lozenges of light as each one lifts his glass,
But I will not give you any idol or idea, creed or king,
I give you the incidental things which pass
Outward through space exactly as each was.

I give you the disproportion between labour spent
And joy at random; the laughter of the Galway sea

Juggling with spars and bones irresponsibly,
I give you the toy Liffey and the vast gulls,
I give you fuchsia hedges and whitewashed walls.

I give you the smell of Norman stone, the squelch
Of bog beneath your boots, the red bog-grass,
The vivid chequer of the Antrim hills, the trough of dark
Golden water for the cart-horses, the brass
Belt of serene sun upon the lough.

And I give you the faces, not the permanent masks,
But the faces balanced in the toppling wave—
His glint of joy in cunning as the farmer asks
Twenty per cent too much, or a girl's, forgetting to be
    suave,
A tiro choosing stuffs, preferring mauve.

And I give you the sea and yet again the sea's
Tumultuous marble,
With Thor's thunder or taking his ease akimbo
Lumbering torso, but finger-tips a marvel
Of surgeon's accuracy.

I would like to give you more but I cannot hold
This stuff within my hands and the train goes on;
I know there are further syntheses to which,
As you have perhaps, people at last attain
And find that they are rich and breathing gold.

                                        [1934]

INTIMATIONS OF MORTALITY

The shadows of the banisters march march,
The lovers linger under the arch,
On the beach the waves creep,
The little boy cannot go to sleep.

He is afraid of God and the Devil—
If he shuts his eyes they will draw level,
So he watches the half-open door and waits
For people on the stairs carrying lights.

Someone comes, carrying a lamp,
The shadows of the banisters march march,
All is above board, order is restored,
Time on horseback under a Roman arch.

Then the final darkness for eight hours
The murderous grin of toothy flowers,
The tick of his pulse in the pillow, the sick
Vertigo of falling in a fanged pit.

After one perfunctory kiss
His parents snore in conjugal bliss.
The night watchman with crossed thumbs
Grows an idol. The Kingdom comes. . . .

[1935]

WOLVES

I do not want to be reflective any more
Envying and despising unreflective things
Finding pathos in dogs and undeveloped handwriting
And young girls doing their hair and all the castles of
    sand
Flushed, by the children's bedtime, level with the shore.

The tide comes in and goes out again, I do not want
To be always stressing either its flux or its permanence,
I do not want to be a tragic or philosophic chorus
But to keep my eye only on the nearer future
And after that let the sea flow over us.

Come then all of you, come closer, form a circle
Join hands and make believe that joined
Hands will keep away the wolves of water
Who howl along our coast. And be it assumed
That no one hears them among the talk and laughter.

[1934]

AUBADE

Having bitten on life like a sharp apple
Or, playing it like a fish, been happy,

Having felt with fingers that the sky is blue,
What have we after that to look forward to?

Not the twilight of the gods but a precise dawn
Of sallow and grey bricks, and newsboys crying war.

[1934]

SNOW

The room was suddenly rich and the great bay-window
    was
Spawning snow and pink roses against it
Soundlessly collateral and incompatible:
World is suddener than we fancy it.

World is crazier and more of it than we think,
Incorrigibly plural. I peel and portion
A tangerine and spit the pips and feel
The drunkenness of things being various.

And the fire flames with a bubbling sound for world
Is more spiteful and gay than one supposes—
On the tongue on the eyes on the ears in the palms of
    your hands—
There is more than glass between the snow and the huge
    roses.

[1935]

41

III

LONGER POEMS

ECLOGUE FOR CHRISTMAS

A. I meet you in an evil time.
B.   The evil bells
   Put out of our heads, I think, the thought of every-
      thing else.
A. The jaded calendar revolves,
   The nuts need oil, carbon chokes the valves,
   The excess sugar of a diabetic culture
   Rotting the nerve of life and literature;
   Therefore when we bring out the old tinsel and frills
   To announce that Christ is born among the barbarous
      hills
   I turn to you whom a morose routine
   Saves from the mad vertigo of being what has been.
B. Analogue of me, you are wrong to turn to me,
   My country will not yield you any sanctuary,
   There is no pinpoint in any of the ordnance maps
   To save you when your towns and town-bred
      thoughts collapse,
   It is better to die *in situ* as I shall,
   One place is as bad as another. Go back where your
      instincts call
   And listen to the crying of the town-cats and the taxis
      again,
   Or wind your gramophone and eavesdrop on great
      men.
A. Jazz-weary of years of drums and Hawaiian guitar,
   Pivoting on the parquet I seem to have moved far
   From bombs and mud and gas, have stuttered on my
      feet

Clinched to the streamlined and butter-smooth trulls
　　of the élite,
The lights irritating and gyrating and rotating in
　　gauze—
Pomade-dazzle, a slick beauty of gewgaws—
I who was Harlequin in the childhood of the century,
Posed by Picasso beside an endless opaque sea,
Have seen myself sifted and splintered in broken
　　facets,
Tentative pencillings, endless liabilities, no assets,
Abstractions scalpelled with a palette-knife
Without reference to this particular life.
And so it has gone on; I have not been allowed to be
Myself in flesh or face, but abstracting and dissecting
　　me
They have made of me pure form, a symbol or a
　　pastiche,
Stylised profile, anything but soul and flesh:
And that is why I turn this jaded music on
To forswear thought and become an automaton.
B. There are in the country also of whom I am afraid—
　　Men who put beer into a belly that is dead,
　　Women in the forties with terrier and setter who
　　　　whistle and swank
　　Over down and plough and Roman road and daisied
　　　　bank,
　　Half-conscious that these barriers over which they
　　　　stride
　　Are nothing to the barbed wire that has grown round
　　　　their pride.
A. And two there are, as I drive in the city, who suddenly
　　perturb—

The one sirening me to draw up by the kerb
The other, as I lean back, my right leg stretched
    creating speed,
Making me catch and stamp, the brakes shrieking,
    pull up dead:
She wears silk stockings taunting the winter wind,
He carries a white stick to mark that he is blind.
B. In the country they are still hunting, in the heavy
    shires
    Greyness is on the fields and sunset like a line of pyres
    Of barbarous heroes smoulders through the ancient
        air
    Hazed with factory dust and, orange opposite, the
        moon's glare,
    Goggling yokel-stubborn through the iron trees,
    Jeers at the end of us, our bland ancestral ease;
    We shall go down like palaeolithic man
    Before some new Ice Age or Genghiz Khan.
A. It is time for some new coinage, people have got so
    old,
    Hacked and handled and shiny from pocketing they
        have made bold
    To think that each is himself through these accidents,
        being blind
    To the fact that they are merely the counters of an
        unknown Mind.
B. A Mind that does not think, if such a thing can be,
    Mechanical Reason, capricious Identity.
    That I could be able to face this domination nor
        flinch—
A. The tin toys of the hawker move on the pavement
    inch by inch

Not knowing that they are wound up; it is better to
   be so
Than to be, like us, wound up and while running
   down to know—
B. But everywhere the pretence of individuality recurs—
A. Old faces frosted with powder and choked in furs.
B. The jutlipped farmer gazing over the humpbacked
   wall.
A. The commercial traveller joking in the urinal—
B. I think things draw to an end, the soil is stale.
A. And over-elaboration will nothing now avail,
   The street is up again, gas, electricity or drains,
   Ever-changing conveniences, nothing comfortable
   remains
   Unimproved, as flagging Rome improved villa and
   sewer
   (A sound-proof library and a stable temperature).
   Our street is up, red lights sullenly mark
   The long trench of pipes, iron guts in the dark,
   And not till the Goths again come swarming down the
   hill
   Will cease the clangour of the pneumatic drill.
   But yet there is beauty narcotic and deciduous
   In this vast organism grown out of us:
   On all the traffic-islands stand white globes like
   moons,
   The city's haze is clouded amber that purrs and
   croons,
   And tilting by the noble curve bus after tall bus comes
   With an osculation of yellow light, with a glory like
   chrysanthemums.

48

B. The country gentry cannot change, they will die in
    their shoes
  From angry circumstance and moral self-abuse,
  Dying with a paltry fizzle they will prove their lives
    to be
  An ever-diluted drug, a spiritual tautology.
  They cannot live once their idols are turned out,
  None of them can endure, for how could they, pos-
    sibly, without
  The flotsam of private property, pekinese and poly-
    anthus,
  The good things which in the end turn to poison and
    pus,
  Without the bandy chairs and the sugar in the silver
    tongs
  And the inter-ripple and resonance of years of dinner-
    gongs?
  Or if they could find no more that cumulative proof
  In the rain dripping off the conservatory roof?
  What will happen when the only sanction the coun-
    try-dweller has—
A. What will happen to us, planked and panelled with
    jazz?
  Who go to the theatre where a black man dances like
    an eel,
  Where pink thighs flash like the spokes of a wheel,
    where we feel
  That we know in advance all the jogtrot and the cake-
    walk jokes,
  All the bumfun and the gags of the comedians in
    boaters and toques,

All the tricks of the virtuosos who invert the usual—
B. What will happen to us when the State takes down
       the manor wall,
   When there is no more private shooting or fishing,
       when the trees are all cut down,
   When faces are all dials and cannot smile or frown—
A. What will happen when the sniggering machine-guns
       in the hands of the young men
   Are trained on every flat and club and beauty parlour
       and Father's den?
   What will happen when our civilisation like a long
       pent balloon—
B. What will happen will happen; the whore and the
       buffoon
   Will come off best; no dreamers, they cannot lose
       their dream
   And are at least likely to be reinstated in the new
       régime.
   But one thing is not likely—
A.   Do not gloat over yourself
   Do not be your own vulture; high on some mountain
       shelf
   Huddle the pitiless abstractions bald about the neck
   Who will descend when you crumple in the plains a
       wreck.
   Over the randy of the theatre and cinema I hear songs
   Unlike anything—
B.   The lady of the house poises the silver tongs
   And picks a lump of sugar, 'ne plus ultra' she says
   'I cannot do otherwise, even to prolong my days'—
A. I cannot do otherwise either, to-night I will book my
       seat—

B. I will walk about the farm-yard which is replete
   As with the smell of dung so with memories—
A. I will gorge myself to satiety with the oddities
   Of every artiste, official or amateur,
   Who has pleased me in my rôle of hero-worshipper
   Who has pleased me in my rôle of individual man—
B. Let us lie once more, say 'What we think, we can'
   The old idealist lie—
A.   And for me before I die
   Let me go the round of the garish glare—
B.   And on the bare and high
   Places of England, the Wiltshire Downs and the Long
     Mynd
   Let the balls of my feet bounce on the turf, my face
     burn in the wind
   My eyelashes stinging in the wind, and the sheep like
     grey stones
   Humble my human pretensions—
A.   Let the saxophones and the xylophones
   And the cult of every technical excellence, the miles
     of canvas in the galleries
   And the canvas of the rich man's yacht snapping and
     tacking on the seas
   And the perfection of a grilled steak—
B.   Let all these so ephemeral things
   Be somehow permanent like the swallow's tangent
     wings:
   Good-bye to you, this day remember is Christmas,
     this morn
   They say, interpret it your own way, Christ is born.
                                             [1933]

51

ECLOGUE BY A FIVE-BARRED GATE

(Death and two Shepherds)

D. There is no way here, shepherds, read the wooden
sign,
Your road is a blind road, all this land is mine.
1. But your fields, mister, would do well for our sheep.
2. They could shelter from the sun where the low hills
dip.
D. I have sheep of my own, see them over there.
1. There seems no nater in 'em, they look half dead.
2. They be no South Downs, they look so thin and bare.
D. More than half, shepherds, they are more than half
dead.
But where are your own flocks you have been so talking of?
1. Right here at our elbow—
2. Or they *was* so just now.
D. That's right, shepherd, they was so just now.
Your sheep are gone, they can't speak for you,
I must have your credentials, sing me who you are.
1. I am a shepherd of the Theocritean breed,
Been pasturing my songs, man and boy, this thirty
year—
2. And for me too my pedigree acceptances
Have multiplied beside the approved streams.
D. This won't do, shepherds, life is not like that,
And when it comes to death I may say he is not like
that.
Have you never thought of Death?
1. Only off and on,

Thanatos in Greek, the accent proparoxytone—
2. That's not what he means, he means the thing behind
     the word
Same as took Alice White the time her had her third—
D. Cut out for once the dialect and the pedantry,
I thought a shepherd was a poet—
1.   On his flute—
2.   On his oat—
D. I thought he was a poet and could quote the prices
Of significant living and decent dying, could lay the
     rails level on the sleepers
To carry the powerful train of abstruse thought—
1. What an idea!
2.   But certainly poets are sleepers,
The sleeping beauty behind the many-coloured
    ·hedge—
D. All you do is burke the other and terrible beauty, all
     you do is hedge
And shirk the inevitable issue, all you do
Is shear your sheep to stop your ears.
Poetry you think is only the surface vanity,
The painted nails, the hips narrowed by fashion,
The hooks and eyes of words; but it is not that only,
And it is not only the curer sitting by the wayside,
Phials on his trestle, his palms grown thin as wafers
With blessing the anonymous heads;
And poetry is not only the bridging of two-banked
     rivers.
2. Whoever heard of a river without a further bank?
D. You two never heard of it.
Tell me now, I have heard the cuckoo, there is tar on
     your shoes,

I surmise that spring is here—
2.   Spring be here truly,
On Bank Holiday I wore canvas shoes,
Could feel the earth—
D.   And that being so, tell me
Don't you ever feel old?
2.   There's a question now.
1.   It is a question we all have to answer,
     And I may say that when I smell the beans or hear
          the thrush
     I feel a wave intensely bitter-sweet and topped with
          silver—
D.   There you go again, your self-congratulation
     Blunts all edges, insulates with wool,
     No spark of reality possible.
     Can't you peel off for even a moment that conscious
          face?
     All time is not your tear-off jotter, you cannot afford
          to scribble
     So many so false answers.
     This escapism of yours is blasphemy;
     An immortal cannot blaspheme for one way or an-
          other
     His trivialities will pattern in the end;
     But for you your privilege and panic is to be mortal
     And with Here and Now for your anvil
     You must strike while the iron is hot—
2.   He is an old man,
     That is why he talks so.
D.   Can't you understand me?
     Look, I will set you a prize like any of your favourites,
     Like any Tityrus or tired Damon;

54

Sing me, each in turn, what dream you had last night
And if either's dream rings true, to him I will open
    my gate:
2. Ho, here's talking.
1.   Let me collect myself.
D. Collect yourself in time for if you win my prize—
2. I'm going to sing first, I had a rare dream.
1. Your dream is nothing—
D.   The more nothing the better.
1. My dream will word well—
2.   But not wear well—
D. No dreams wear at all as dreams.
    Water appears tower only while in well—
    All from the same comes, the same drums sound
    In the pulsation of all the bulging suns,
    And no clock whatever, while winding or running
        down,
    Makes any difference to time however the long-
        legged weights
    Straggle down the cottage wall or the child grows
        leggy too—
1. I do not like your talking.
2.   It gives giddiness
    Like the thrumming of the telephone wires in an
        east wind
    With the bellyache and headache and nausea.
D. It is not my nature to talk, so sing your pieces
    And I will try, what is repugnant too, to listen.
1. Last night as the bearded lips of sleep
    Closed with the slightest sigh on me and I sank
        through the blue soft caves
    Picked with light delicate as the chink of coins

Or stream on the pebbles I was caught by hands
And a face was swung in my eyes like a lantern
Swinging on the neck of a snake.
And that face I knew to be God and I woke,
And now I come to look at yours, stranger,
There is something in the lines of it—
D.   Your dream, shepherd,
Is good enough of its kind. Now let us hear yours.
2. Well, I dreamt it was a hot day, the territorials
Were out on melting asphalt under the howitzers,
The brass music bounced on the houses. Come
I heard cry as it were a water-nymph, come and fulfil
     me
And I sped floating, my feet plashing in the tops of
     the wheat
But my eyes were blind,
I found her with my hands lying on the drying hay,
Wet heat in the deeps of the hay as my hand delved,
And I possessed her, gross and good like the hay,
And she went and my eyes regained sight and the
     sky was full of ladders
Angels ascending and descending with a shine like
     mackerel—
Now I come to tell it it sounds nonsense.
D. Thank you, gentlemen, these two dreams are good,
Better than your daytime madrigals.
If you really wish I will give you both the prize,
But take another look at my land before you choose it.
1. It looks colder now.
2.   The sheep have not moved.
1. I have a fancy there is no loving there
Even among sheep.

56

D.   They do not breed or couple.
1 & 2. And what about us, shall we enjoy it there?
D. *Enjoy what where?*
2.   Why, life in your land.
D. I will open this gate that you may see for yourselves.
1. You go first.
2.   Well, you come too.
1 & 2. We will go together to these pastures new . . .
D. So; they are gone; life in my land . . .
    There is no life as there is no land.
    They are gone and I am alone
    With a gate the façade of a mirage.

                               [1934]

ECLOGUE FROM ICELAND

*Scene: The Arnarvatn Heath. Craven, Ryan and the
ghost of Grettir. Voice from Europe.*

R.   This is the place, Craven, the end of our way;
       Hobble the horses, we have had a long day.
C.   The night is closing like a fist
       And the long glacier lost in mist.
R.   Few folk come this time of year.
       What are those limping steps I hear?
C.   Look, there he is coming now.
       We shall have some company anyhow.
R.   It must be the mist—he looks so big;
       He is walking lame in the left leg.
G.   Good evening, strangers. So you too
       Are on the run? I welcome you.

I am Grettir Asmundson,
Dead many years. My day is done.
But you whose day is sputtering yet
I forget. . . . What did I say?
We forget when we are dead
The blue and red, the grey and gay.
Your day spits with a damp wick,
Will fizzle out if you're not quick.
Men have been chilled to death who kissed
Wives of mist, forgetting their own
Kind who live out of the wind.
My memory goes, goes——Tell me
Are there men now whose compass leads
Them always down forbidden roads?
Greedy young men who take their pick
Of what they want but have no luck;
Who leap the toothed and dour crevasse
Of death on a sardonic phrase?
You with crowsfeet round your eyes
How are things where you come from?

C.   Things are bad. There is no room
To move at ease, to stretch or breed—

G.   And you with the burglar's underlip
In your land do things stand well?

R.   In my land nothing stands at all
But some fly high and some lie low.

G.   Too many people. My memory will go,
Lose itself in the hordes of modern people.
Memory is words; we remember what others
Say and record of ourselves—stones with the
      runes.
Too many people—sandstorm over the words.

Is your land also an island?
There is only hope for people who live upon is-
    lands
Where the Lowest Common labels will not stick
And the unpolluted hills will hold your echo.

R.   I come from an island, Ireland, a nation
Built upon violence and morose vendettas.
My diehard countrymen like drayhorses
Drag their ruin behind them.
Shooting straight in the cause of crooked think-
    ing
Their greed is sugared with pretence of public
    spirit.
From all which I am an exile.

C.   Yes, we are exiles,
Gad the world for comfort.
This Easter I was in Spain before the Civil War
Gobbling the tripper's treats, the local colour,
Storks over Avila, the coffee-coloured waters of
    Ronda,
The comedy of the bootblacks in the cafés,
The legless beggars in the corridors of the trains
Dominoes on marble tables, the architecture
Moorish mudejar churriguerresque,
The bullfight—the banderillas like Christmas can-
    dles,
And the scrawled hammer and sickle:
It was all copy—impenetrable surface.
I did not look for the sneer beneath the surface.
Why should I trouble, an addict to oblivion
Running away from the gods of my own hearth
With no intention of finding gods elsewhere?

R.   And so we came to Iceland—
C.   Our latest joyride.
G.   And what have you found in Iceland?
C.   What have we found? More copy, more surface,
          Vignettes as they call them, dead flowers in an
              album—
          The harmoniums in the farms, the fine-bread and
              pancakes,
          The pot of ivy trained across the window,
          Children in gumboots, girls in black berets.
R.   And dead craters and angled crags.
G.   The crags which saw me jockey doom for twenty
          Years from one cold hide-out to another;
          The last of the saga heroes
          Who had not the wisdom of Njal or the beauty of
              Gunnar
          I was the doomed tough, disaster kept me witty;
          Being born the surly jack, the ne'er-do-well, the
              loiterer
          Hard blows exalted me.
          When the man of will and muscle achieves the
              curule chair
          He turns to a bully; better is his lot as outlaw
          A wad of dried fish in his belt, a snatch of bilber-
              ries
          And riding the sullen landscape far from friends
          Through the jungle of lava, dales of frozen fancy,
          Fording the gletcher, ducking the hard hail,
          And across the easy pastures, never stopping
          To rest among the celandines and bogcotton.
          Under a curse I would see eyes in the night,

Always had to move on; craving company
In the end I lived on an island with two others.
To fetch fire I swam the crinkled fjord,
The crags were alive with ravens whose low croak
Told my ears what filtered in my veins—
The sense of doom. I wore it gracefully,
The fatal clarity that would not budge
But without false pride in martyrdom. For I,
Joker and dandy, held no mystic's pose,
Not wishing to die preferred the daily goods
The horse-fight, women's thighs, a joint of meat.

C.   But this dyspeptic age of ingrown cynics
Wakes in the morning with a coated tongue
And whets itself laboriously to labour
And wears a blasé face in the face of death.
Who risk their lives neither to fill their bellies
Nor to avenge an affront nor grab a prize
But out of bravado or to divert ennui
Driving fast cars and climbing foreign moun-
    tains.
Outside the delicatessen shop the hero
With his ribbons and his empty pinned-up sleeve
Cadges for money while with turned-up collars
His comrades blow through brass the London-
    derry air
And silken legs and swinging buttocks advertise
The sale of little cardboard flags on pins.

G.   Us too they sold
The women and the men with many sheep.
Graft and aggression, legal prevarication
Drove out the best of us,

Secured long life to only the sly and the dumb
To those who would not say what they really
        thought
But got their ends through pretended indiffer-
        ence
And through the sweat and blood of thralls and
        hacks
Cheating the poor men of their share of drift
The whale on Kaldbak in the starving winter.

R. And so today at Grimsby men whose lives
Are warped in Arctic trawlers load and unload
The shining tons of fish to keep the lords
Of the market happy with cigars and cars.

C. What is that music in the air—
Organ-music coming from far?

R. Honeyed music—it sounds to me
Like the Wurlitzer in the Gaiety.

G. I do not hear anything at all.

C. Imagine the purple light on the stage

R. The melting moment of a stinted age

C. The pause before the film again
Bursts in a shower of golden rain.

G. I do not hear anything at all.

C. We shall be back there soon, to stand in queues
For entertainment and to work at desks,
To browse round counters of dead books, to pore
On picture catalogues and Soho menus,
To preen ourselves on the reinterpretation
Of the words of obsolete interpreters,
Collate delete their faded lives like texts,
Admire Flaubert, Cézanne—the tortured artists—

And leaning forward to knock out our pipes
Into the fire protest that art is good
And gives a meaning and a slant to life.

G. The dark is falling. Soon the air
Will stare with eyes, the stubborn ghost
Who cursed me when I threw him. Must
The ban go on for ever? I,
A ghost myself, have no claim now to die.

R. Now I hear the music again—
Strauss and roses—hear it plain.
The sweet confetti of music falls
From the high Corinthian capitals.

C. Her head upon his shoulder lies. . . .
Blend to the marrow as the music dies.

G. Brought up to the rough-house we took offence
quickly
Were sticklers for pride, paid for it as outlaws—

C. Like Cavalcanti whose hot blood lost him Florence

R. Or the Wild Geese of Ireland in Mid-Europe.
Let us thank God for valour in abstraction
For those who go their own way, will not kiss
The arse of law and order nor compound
For physical comfort at the price of pride:
Soldiers of fortune, renegade artists, rebels and
sharpers
Whose speech not cramped to Yea and Nay ex-
plodes
In crimson oaths like peonies, who brag
Because they prefer to taunt the mask of God,
Bid him unmask and die in the living lightning.

63

What is that voice maundering, meandering?

VOICE. Blues . . . blues . . . high heels and mani-
cured hands
Always self-conscious of the vanity bag
And puritan painted lips that abnegate desire
And say 'we do not care' . . . 'we do not care'—
I don't care always in the air
Give my hips a shake always on the make
Always on the mend coming around the bend
Always on the dance with an eye to the main
Chance, always taking the floor again—

C. There was Tchekov,
His haemorrhages drove him out of Moscow
The life he loved, not born to it, who thought
That when the windows blurred with smoke and
talk
So that no one could see out, then conversely
The giants of frost and satans of the peasant
Could not look in, impose the evil eye.

R. There was MacKenna
Spent twenty years translating Greek philosophy
Ill and tormented, unwilling to break contract,
A brilliant talker who left
The salon for the solo flight of Mind.

G. There was Onund Treefoot
Came late and lame to Iceland, made his way
Even though the land was bad and the neigh-
bours jealous.

C. There was that dancer
Who danced the War, then falling into coma
Went with hunched shoulders through the ivory
gate.

64

R.   There was Connolly
            Vilified now by the gangs of Catholic Action.

G.   There was Egil
            Hero and miser who when dying blind
            Would have thrown his money among the crowd
                 to hear
            The whole world scuffle for his hoarded gold.

C.   And there were many
            Whose common sense or sense of humour or mere
            Desire for self assertion won them through

R.   But not to happiness. Though at intervals
            They paused in sunlight for a moment's fusion
            With friends or nature till the cynical wind
            Blew the trees pale—

Voice.   Blues, blues, sit back, relax
            Let your self-pity swell with the music and clutch
            Your tiny lavendered fetishes. Who cares
            If floods depopulate China? I don't care
            Always in the air sitting among the stars
            Among the electric signs among the imported
                 wines
            Always on the spree climbing the forbidden tree
            Tossing the peel of the apple over my shoulder
            To see it form the initials of a new intrigue.

G.   Runes and runes which no one could decode

R.   Wrong numbers on the phone—she never
                answered.

C.   And from the romantic grill (Spanish baroque)
            Only the eyes looked out which I see now.

G.   You see them now?

C.   But seen before as well.

G.   And many times to come, be sure of that.

R. I know them too
    These eyes which hang in the northern mist, the
        brute
    Stare of stupidity and hate, the most
    Primitive and false of oracles.
C.   The eyes
    That glide like snakes behind a thousand masks—
    All human faces fit them, here or here:
    Dictator, bullying schoolboy or common lout,
    Acquisitive women, financiers, invalids,
    Are capable all of that compelling stare
    Stare which betrays the cosmic purposelessness
    The nightmare noise of the scythe upon the hone,
    Time sharpening his blade among high rocks
        alone.
R. The face that fate hangs as a figurehead
    Above the truncheon or the nickelled death.
G. I won the fall. Though cursed for it, I won.
C. Which is why we honour you who working from
    The common premisses did not end with many
    In the blind alley where the trek began.
G. Though the open road is hard with frost and dark.
VOICE. Hot towels for the men, mud packs for the women
    Will smooth the puckered minutes of your lives.
    I offer you each a private window, a view
    (The leper window reveals a church of lepers).
R. Do you believe him?
C. I don't know.
    Do you believe him?
G. No.
    You cannot argue with the eyes or voice;
    Argument will frustrate you till you die

But go your own way, give the voice the lie,
Outstare the inhuman eyes. That is the way.
Go back to where you came from and do not keep
Crossing the road to escape them, do not avoid
    the ambush,
Take sly detours, but ride the pass direct.

C.   But the points of axes shine from the scrub, the
    odds
Are dead against us. There are the lures of
    women
Who, half alive, invite to a fuller life
And never loving would be loved by others.

R.   Who fortify themselves in pasteboard castles
And plant their beds with the cast-out toys of
    children,
Dead pines with tinsel fruits, nursery beliefs
And South Sea Island trinkets. Watch their years
The permutations of lapels and gussets,
Of stuffs—georgette or velvet or corduroy—
Of hats and eye-veils, of shoes, lizard or suède,
Of bracelets, milk or coral, of zip bags
Of compacts, lipstick, eyeshade and coiffures
All tributary to the wished ensemble
The carriage of body that belies the soul.

C.   And there are the men who appear to be men of
    sense,
Good company and dependable in a crisis,
Who yet are ready to plug you as you drink
Like dogs who bite from fear; for fear of germs
Putting on stamps by licking the second finger,
For fear of opinion overtipping in bars,
For fear of thought studying stupefaction.

It is the world which these have made where dead
Greek words sprout out in tin on sallow walls—
Clinic or polytechnic—a world of slums
Where any day now may see the Gadarene swine
Rush down the gullets of the London tubes
When the enemy, x or y, let loose their gas.

G.   My friends, hounded like me, I tell you still
Go back where you belong. I could have fled
To the Hebrides or Orkney, been rich and fa-
      mous,
Preferred to assert my rights in my own country,
Mine which were hers for every country stands
By the sanctity of the individual will.

R.   Yes, he is right.

C.   But we have not his strength

R.   Could only abase ourselves before the wall
Of shouting flesh

C.   Could only offer our humble
Deaths to the unknown god, unknown but wor-
      shipped,
Whose voice calls in the sirens of destroyers.

G.   Minute your gesture but it must be made—
Your hazard, your act of defiance and hymn of
      hate,
Hatred of hatred, assertion of human values,
Which is now your only duty.

C.   Is it our only duty?

G.   Yes, my friends.
What did you say? The night falls now and I
Must beat the dales to chase my remembered
      acts.

Yes, my friends, it is your only duty.
And, it may be added, it is your only chance.

[1936]

ECLOGUE BETWEEN THE MOTHERLESS

A.   What did you do for the holiday?
B.   I went home.
      What did you do?
A.   O, I went home for the holiday.
      Had a good time?
B.   Not bad as far as it went.
      What about you?
A.   O quite a good time on the whole—
(both) Quite a good time on the whole at home for the
        holiday—
A.   As far as it went—In a way it went too far,
      Back to childhood, back to the backwoods mind;
      I could not stand a great deal of it, bars on the
        brain
      And the blinds drawn in the drawingroom not to
        fade the chair covers
B.   There were no blinds drawn in ours; my father
        has married again—
      A girl of thirty who had never had any lovers
      And wants to have everything bright
A.   That sounds worse than us.
      Our old house is just a grass-grown tumulus,
      My father sits by himself with the bossed de-
        canter,

69

The garden is going to rack, the gardener
Only comes three days, most of our money was in
    linen

B.   My new stepmother is wealthy, you should see
    her in jodhpurs
Brisking in to breakfast from a morning canter.
I don't think he can be happy

A.   How can you tell?
That generation is so different

B.   I suppose your sister
Still keeps house for yours?

A.   Yes and she finds it hell.
Nothing to do in the evenings.

B.   Talking of the evenings
I can drop the ash on the carpet since my divorce.
Never you marry, my boy. One marries only
Because one thinks one is lonely—and so one was
But wait till the lonely are two and no better

A.   As a matter
Of fact I've got to tell you

B.   The first half year
Is heaven come back from the nursery—swans-
    down kisses—
But after that one misses something

A.   My dear,
Don't depress me in advance; I've got to tell you—

B.   My wife was warmth, a picture and a dance,
Her body electric—silk used to crackle and her
    gloves
Move where she left them. How one loves the
    surface

But how one lacks the core—Children of course
Might make a difference
A.   Personally I find
I cannot go on any more like I was. Which is why
I took this step in the dark
B.   What step?
A.   I thought
I too might try what you
B.   Don't say that you
And after all this time
A.   Let's start from the start.
When I went home this time there was nothing
   to do
And so I got haunted. Like a ball of wool
That kittens have got at, all my growing up
All the disposed-of process of my past
Unravelled on the floor—One can't proceed any
   more
Except on a static past; when the ice-floe breaks
What's the good of walking? Talking of ice
I remembered my mother standing against the
   sky
And saying 'Go back in the house and change
   your shoes'
And I kept having dreams and kept going back
   in the house.
A sense of guilt like a scent—The day I was born
I suppose that that same hour was full of her
   screams
B.   You're run down
A.   Wait till you hear what I've done.

71

It was not only dreams; even the crockery (odd
It's not all broken by now) and the rustic seat in
    the rockery
With the bark flaked off, all kept reminding me,
    binding
My feet to the floating past. In the night at the
    lodge
A dog was barking as when I was little in the
    night
And I could not budge in the bed clothes. Lying
    alone
I felt my legs were paralysed into roots
And the same cracks in what used to be the nurs-
    ery ceiling
Gave me again the feeling I was young among
    ikons,
Helpless at the feet of faceless family idols,
Walking the tightrope over the tiger-pit,
Running the gauntlet of inherited fears;
So after all these years I turned in the bed
And grasped the want of a wife and heard in the
    rain
On the gravel path the steps of all my mistresses
And wondered which was coming or was she
    dead
And her shoes given to the char which tapped
    through London—
The black streets mirrored with rain and stained
    with lights.
I dreamed she came while a train
Was running behind the trees (with power pro-
    gressing),

72

Undressing deftly she slipped cool knees beside
    me,
The clipped hair on her neck prickled my tongue
And the whole room swung like a ship till I woke
    with the window
Jittering in its frame from the train passing the
    garden
Carrying its load of souls to a different distance.
And of others, isolated by associations,
I thought—the scent of syringa or always wear-
    ing
A hat of fine white straw and never known in
    winter—
Splinters of memory. When I was little I sorted
Bits of lustre and glass from the heap behind the
    henhouse;
They are all distorted now the beautiful sirens
Mutilated and mute in dream's dissection,
Hanged from pegs in the Bluebeard's closet of
    the brain,
Never again nonchalantly to open
The doors of disillusion. Whom recording
The night marked time, the dog at the lodge kept
    barking
And as he barked the big cave opened of hell
Where all their voices were one and stuck at a
    point
Like a gramophone needle stuck on a notched
    record.
I thought 'Can I find a love beyond the family
And feed her to the bed my mother died in
Between the tallboys and the vase of honesty

On which I was born and groped my way from
    the cave
With a half-eaten fruit in my hand, a passport
    meaning
Enforced return for periods to that country?
Or will one's wife also belong to that country
And can one never find the perfect stranger?

B.   My complaint was that she stayed a stranger.
I remember her mostly in the car, stopping by the
    white
Moons of the petrol pumps, in a camelhair rug
Comfortable, scented and alien.

A.   That's what I want,
Someone immutably alien—
Send me a woman with haunches out of the
    jungle
And frost patterns for fancies
The hard light of sun upon water in diamonds
    dancing
And the brute swagger of the sea; let her love be
    the drop
From the cliff of my dream, be the axe on the
    block
Be finesse of the ice on the panes of the heart
Be careless, be callous, be glass frolic of prisms
Be eyes of guns through lashes of barbed wire,
Be the gaoler's smile and all that breaks the past.

B.   Odd ideals you have; all I wanted
Was to get really close but closeness was
Only a glove on the hand, alien and veinless,
And yet her empty gloves could move

A.   My next move

74

Is what I've got to tell you, I picked on the only
One who would suit and wrote proposing marriage

B.   Who is she?

A.   But she can't have yet received it;
She is in India.

B.   India be damned.
What is her name?

A.   I said I cannot offer
Anything you will want

B.   Why?

A.   and I said
I know in two years' time it will make no differ-
ence.
I was hardly able to write it at the claw-foot
table
Where my mother kept her diary. There I sat
Concocting a gambler's medicine; the afternoon
was cool,
The ducks drew lines of white on the dull slate
of the pool
And I sat writing to someone I hardly knew
And someone I shall never know well. Relying on
that
I stuck up the envelope, walked down the wind-
ing drive,
All that was wanted a figurehead, passed by the
lodge
Where the dog is chained and the gates, relying
on my mood
To get it posted

B.   Who is the woman?

A.   relying
B.   Who is the woman?
A.   She is dying
B.   Dying of what?
A.   Only a year to live
B.   Forgive me asking
          But
A.   Only a year and ten yards down the road
          I made my goal where it has always stood
          Waiting for the last
B.   You must be out of your mind;
          If it were anyone else I should not mind
A.   Waiting for the last collection before dark
          The pillarbox like an exclamation mark.

                                                [1937]

VALEDICTION

Their verdure dare not show . . . their verdure dare
     not show . . .
Cant and randy—the seals' heads bobbing in the tide-
     flow
Between the islands, sleek and black and irrelevant
They cannot depose logically what they want:
Died by gunshot under borrowed pennons,
Sniped from the wet gorse and taken by the limp fins
And slung like a dead seal in a boghole, beaten up
By peasants with long lips and the whisky-drinker's
     cough.
Park your car in the city of Dublin, see Sackville Street
Without the sandbags in the old photos, meet

The statues of the patriots, history never dies,
At any rate in Ireland, arson and murder are legacies
Like old rings hollow-eyed without their stones
Dumb talismans.
See Belfast, devout and profane and hard,
Built on reclaimed mud, hammers playing in the ship-
    yard;
Time punched with holes like a steel sheet, time
Hardening the faces, veneering with a grey and speckled
    rime
The faces under the shawls and caps:
This was my mother-city, these my paps.
Country of callous lava cooled to stone,
Of minute sodden haycocks, of ship-sirens' moan,
Of falling intonations—I would call you to book
I would say to you, Look;
I would say, This is what you have given me
Indifference and sentimentality
A metallic giggle, a fumbling hand
A heart that leaps to a fife band:
Set these against your water-shafted air
Of amethyst and moonstone, the horses' feet like bells of
    hair
Shambling beneath the orange-cart, the beer-brown
    spring
Guzzling between the heather, the green gush of Irish
    spring.
Cursèd be he that curses his mother. I cannot be
Anyone else than what this land engendered me:
In the back of my mind are snips of white, the sails
Of the Lough's fishing-boats, the bellropes lash their tails
When I would peal my thoughts, the bells pull free—

Memory in apostasy.
I would tot up my factors
But who can stand in the way of his soul's steam-
tractors?
I can say Ireland is hooey, Ireland is
A gallery of fake tapestries,
But I cannot deny my past to which my self is wed,
The woven figure cannot undo its thread.
On a cardboard lid I saw when I was four
Was the trade-mark of a hound and a round tower,
And that was Irish glamour, and in the cemetery
Sham Celtic crosses claimed our individuality,
And my father talked about the West where years back
He played hurley on the sands with a stick of wrack.
Park your car in Killarney, buy a souvenir
Of green marble or black bog-oak, run up to Clare,
Climb the cliff in the postcard, visit Galway city,
Romanticise on our Spanish blood, leave ten per cent of
pity
Under your plate for the emigrant,
Take credit for our sanctity, our heroism and our sterile
want
Columba Kevin and briny Brandan the accepted names,
Wolfe Tone and Grattan and Michael Collins the
accepted names,
Admire the suavity with which the architect
Is rebuilding the burnt mansion, recollect
The palmy days of the Horse Show, swank your fill,
But take the Holyhead boat before you pay the bill;
Before you face the consequence
Of inbred soul and climatic maleficence
And pay for the trick beauty of a prism
78

In drug-dull fatalism.
I will exorcise my blood
And not to have my baby-clothes my shroud
I will acquire an attitude not yours
And become as one of your holiday visitors,
And however often I may come
Farewell, my country, and in perpetuum;
Whatever desire I catch when your wind scours my face
I will take home and put in a glass case
And merely look on
At each new fantasy of badge and gun.
Frost will not touch the hedge of fuchsias,
The land will remain as it was,
But no abiding content can grow out of these minds
Fuddled with blood, always caught by blinds;
The eels go up the Shannon over the great dam;
You cannot change a response by giving it a new name.
Fountain of green and blue curling in the wind
I must go east and stay, not looking behind,
Not knowing on which day the mist is blanket-thick
Nor when sun quilts the valley and quick
Winging shadows of white clouds pass
Over the long hills like a fiddle's phrase.
If I were a dog of sunlight I would bound
From Phoenix Park to Achill Sound,
Picking up the scent of a hundred fugitives
That have broken the mesh of ordinary lives,
But being ordinary too I must in course discuss
What we mean to Ireland or Ireland to us;
I have to observe milestone and curio
The beaten buried gold of an old king's bravado,
Falsetto antiquities, I have to gesture,

Take part in, or renounce, each imposture;
Therefore I resign, good-bye the chequered and the
    quiet hills
The gaudily-striped Atlantic, the linen-mills
That swallow the shawled file, the black moor where
    half
A turf-stack stands like a ruined cenotaph;
Good-bye your hens running in and out of the white
    house
Your absent-minded goats along the road, your black
    cows
Your greyhounds and your hunters beautifully bred
Your drums and your dolled-up Virgins and your ig-
    norant dead.

[1934]

ODE

To-night is so coarse with chocolate
        The wind blowing from Bournville
That I hanker after the Atlantic
        With a frivolous nostalgia
Like that which film-fans feel
        For their celluloid abstractions
The nifty hero and the deathless blonde
        And find escape by proxy
From the eight-hour day or the wheel
        Of work and bearing children.

If God is boundless as the sea or sky
The eye bounds both of them and Him,

80

We always have the horizon
Not to swim to but to see:
God is seen with shape and limit
More purple towards the rim,
This segment of His infinite extension
Is all the God of Him for me.

And you too, my love, my limit,
So palpable and your hair shot with red—
I do not want a hundred wives or lives
Any more than I want to be too well-read
Or have money like the sand or ability like the hydra's
          heads
To flicker the tongues of self-engendering power,
I want a sufficient sample, the exact and framed
Balance of definite masses, the islanded hour.

I would pray for that island; mob mania in the air,
I cannot assume their easy bravery
Drugged with a slogan, chewing the old lie
That parallel lines will meet at infinity;
As I walk on the shore of the regular and rounded sea
I would pray off from my son the love of that infinite
Which is too greedy and too obvious; let his Absolute
Like any four-walled house be put up decently.

Let us turn to homeliness,
Born in the middle of May
Let him accumulate, corroborate while he may
The blessedness of fact
Which lives in the dancing atom and the breathing trees
And everywhere except in the fancy of man
Who daubs his slush on the hawthorn and the may.

Let him have five good senses
The feeling for symmetry
And the sense of the magnet,
His mind deft and unflustered
To change gear easily
And let not the blasphemy
Of dusty words deceive him.

May he hit the golden mean
Which contains the seasonal extreme.
May he riot in the diving sun
And die in the crystal dream,
May his good deeds flung forth
Like boomerangs return
To wear around his neck
As beads of definite worth.

May he pick up daintily
The ambiguous joys,
As a bee in May the blossom of fruit
Cross-fertilise his data and distil
From the drum balalaika fiddle and organ
From sun's gunnery splintering glass
More than the twanging dazzle or the dazzling noise.

To get permanence, to hear the personance
Of all the water-gullies and blackbirds' songs
Drained off or died twenty years back
To make his flesh of them and so renounce the mask
Of the sham soul, the cask bobbing empty
On leaden waves, the veneer the years crack.

To ride two horses at once, a foot on each
Tilting outward on space abstract and packed
With the audience of the dead and the unborn,
To pay his debts to each
To beach his boat so that others can use it
To throw his bread on the waters, the best deposit.

That people are lovable is a strange discovery
And there are many conflicting allegiances;
The pedals of a chance bicycle
Make a gold shower turning in the sun,
Trains leave in all directions on wild rails
And for every act determined on and won
There is a possible world denied and lost.

Do not then turn maudlin or weathercock,
We must cut the throat of the hour
That it may not haunt us because our sentiments
Continued its existence to pollute
Its essence; bottled time turns sour upon the sill.
The children play in the park; the ducklings
Rise and scurry on the water, a car
Changes down, the sandwichmen
Move up and down with the never-changing news.
Do not brood too much on the forking paths.

The leaves dark green on top, light green under, seas of
    green
Had brought him on full flood, the colour laid on in slices
As by a mason's trowel or ice cream in sliders
Bought in dusty streets under the yellow-green beeches,

A little while ago the green was only peppered
But now we gape at a wealthy wave and a tidal tower
        of green.

Coral azalea and scarlet rhododendron
Syringa and pink horse-chestnut and laburnum
Solid as temples, niched with the song of birds,
Widen the eyes and nostrils, demand homage of words.
And we have to turn from them,
Compose ourselves, fit out an ethic:
Have I anything to hand my son,
Scarab or compass for his journey?

Only so far, so far as I can find, symbols;
No decalogue, no chemical formula;
Unanalysed scent and noise, the fly on the pane,
The tulips banked on the glass-and-black hearse
A memory of a cock crowing in the dark like a curse
The remembered hypnotism of an aeroplane in June—

Watching the cricket from between
Slabs of green and slabs of blue and slowly ladled clouds
We looked at the sky through straw hats,
The sky was turned into black and white small stars.
Then came, southward as always, the angel
His song like the heat dancing on the gravel
High above the bat-chock and the white umpires
Moving south while the clapping of a run turns chill in
        echo
And his own drone is whittled to the point of a pin
So that dozing boys fumble the ghost of sound.

But this identical sound the then epitome
Of summer's athletic ease and the smell of cut grass
Will sometime be our augury of war
When these tiny flies like nibs will calmly draw our death
A dipping gradient on the graph of Europe
And over the hairy flatnesses of Russia
This sound when we have died will linger to a wisp
And the endless corn wave tiredly.

Humming and buzzing, the bomber and the fly on the
            pane
And the telephone wires hung on dead pines,
In Ireland once a string of bright-red haws
Hung, thrown up by children, on those wires:
Not to hang so, O God, between your iron spires!
The town-dweller like a rabbit in a greengrocer's
Who was innocent and integral once
Now, red with slit guts, hangs by the heels
Hangs by the heels gut-open against the fog
Between two spires that are not conscious of him.

Therefore let not my son, halving the truth
Be caught between jagged edges;
And let him not falsify the world
By taking it to pieces;
The marriage of Cause and Effect, Form and Content
Let him not part asunder.
Wisdom for him in the time of tulips
Monastic repose, martial élan,
Then the opening mouth a dragon or a voluptuary—
These moments let him retain like limbs
His time not crippled by flaws of faith or memory.

In the Birmingham Market Hall at this time
There are horseshoe wreaths of mauve stock
Fixed with wire and nailed with pale pink roses
The tribute to a life that ran on standard wheels—
May his life be more than this matter of wheels and wire.

I remember all the houses where parents
Have reared their children to be parents
(Cut box and privet and the parrot's voice)
To be clerks to total the flow of alien money
To be florists to design these wreaths and wedding
          bouquets.

I cannot draw up any code
      There are too many qualifications
Too many asterisk asides
      Too many crosses in the margin
But as others, forgetting the others,
      Run after the nostrums
Of science art and religion
      So would I mystic and maudlin
Dream of the both real and ideal
      Breakers of ocean.
I must put away this drug.

Must become the migrating bird following felt routes
The comet's superficially casual orbit kept
Not self-abandoning to sky-blind chutes
To climb miles and kiss the miles of foam
For nothing is more proud than humbly to accept
And without soaring or swerving win by ignoring
The endlessly curving sea and so come to one's home.

And so come to one's peace while the yellow waves are
    roaring.

                                                 [1934]

HOMAGE TO CLICHÉS

With all this clamour for progress
This hammering out of new phases and gadgets, new
    trinkets and phrases
I prefer the automatic, the reflex, the cliché of velvet.
The foreseen smile, sexual, maternal, or hail-fellow-met
The cat's fur sparking under your hand
The indolent delicacy of your hand
These fish coming in to the net
I can see them coming for yards
The way that you answer, the way that you dangle your
    foot
These fish that are rainbow and fat
One can catch in the hand and caress and return to the
    pool.
So five minutes spent at a bar
Watching the fish coming in, as you parry and shrug
This is on me or this is on me,
Or an old man momentously sharpens a pencil as though
He were not merely licking his fur like a cat—
The cat's tongue curls to the back of its neck, the fish
    swivel round by the side of their tails, on the abbey
    the arrows of gold
On the pinnacles shift in the wind—

This is on me this time
Watch how your flattery logic seduction or wit
Elicit the expected response
Each tiny hammer of the abbey chime
Beating on the outer shell of the eternal bell
Which hangs like a Rameses, does not deign to move
For Mahomet comes to the mountain and the fish come
    to the bell.
What will you have now? The same again?
A finger can pull these ropes,
A gin and lime or a double Scotch
Watch the response, the lifting wrist the clink and smile
The fish come in, the hammered notes come out
From a filigree gothic trap.
These are the moments that are anaplerotic, these are
    the gifts to be accepted
Remembering the qualification
That everything is not true to type like these
That the pattern and the patina of these
Are superseded in the end.
Stoop your head, follow me through this door
Up the belfry stair.
What do you see in this gloom, this womb of stone?
I see eight bells hanging alone.
Eight black panthers, eight silences
On the outer shell of which our fingers via hammers
Rapping with an impertinent precision
Have made believe that this was the final music.
Final as if finality were the trend of fish
That always seek the net
As if finality were the obvious gag
The audience laughing in anticipation

As if finality were the angled smile
Drawn from the dappled stream of casual meetings
(Yet oh thank God for such)
But there is this much left over
There is very much left over:
The Rameses, the panther, the two-ton bell
Will never move his sceptre
Never spring, never swing
No, no, he will never move. . .
What will you have, my dear? The same again?
Two more double Scotch, watch the approved response
This is the preferred mode
I have shut the little window that looks up the road
Towards the tombs of the kings
For I have heard that you meet people walking in granite
I have shut up the gates under padlock
For fear of wild beasts
And I have shut my ears to the possible peal of bells,
Every precaution—
What will you have, my dear? The same again?
Count up our fag-ends
This year next year sometime never
Next year is this year, sometime is next time, never is
      sometime
Never is the Bell, Never is the Panther, Never is Rameses
Oh the cold stone panic of Never—
The ringers are taking off their coats, the panther
      crouches
The granite sceptre is very slightly inclining
As our shoes tap against the bar and our glasses
Make two new rings of wet upon the counter
Somewhere behind us stands a man, a counter

A timekeeper with a watch and a pistol
Ready to shoot and with his shot destroy
This whole delightful world of cliché and refrain—
What will you have, my dear? The same again?

[1935]

LETTER TO GRAHAM AND ANNA

Reykjavik
August 16, 1936

To Graham and Anna: from the Arctic Gate
I send this letter to N. W. 8,
Hoping that Town is not the usual mess,
That Pauli is rid of worms, the new cook a success.
I have got here, you see, without being sick
On a boat of eight hundred tons to Reykjavik.
Came second-class—no air but many men;
Having seen the first-class crowd would do the same
        again.
Food was good, mutton and bits of fishes,
A smart line-up of Scandinavian dishes—
Beet, cheese, ham, jam, smoked salmon, gaffalbitar,
Sweet cucumber, German sausage, and Rye-Vita.
So I came here to the land the Romans missed,
Left for the Irish saint and the Viking colonist.
But what am I doing here? Qu'allais-je faire
Among these volcanic rocks and this grey air?
Why go north when Cyprus and Madeira
De jure if not de facto are much nearer?
The reason for hereness seems beyond conjecture,

There are no trees or trains or architecture,
Fruits and greens are insufficient for health,
Culture is limited by lack of wealth,
The tourist sights have nothing like Stonehenge,
The literature is all about revenge.
And yet I like it if only because this nation
Enjoys a scarcity of population
And cannot rise to many bores or hacks
Or paupers or poor men paying Super-Tax.
Yet further, if you can stand it, I will set forth
The obscure but powerful ethics of Going North.
Morris did it before, dropping the frills and fuss,
Harps and arbours, Tristram and Theseus,
For a land of rocks and sagas. And certain unknown
Old Irish hermits, holy skin and bone,
Camped on these crags in order to forget
Their blue-black cows in Kerry pastures wet.
Those Latin-chattering margin-illuminating monks
Fled here from home without kit-bags or trunks
To mortify their flesh—but we must mortify
Our blowsy intellects before we die,
Who feed our brains on backchat and self-pity
And always need a noise, the radio or the city,
Traffic and changing lights, crashing the amber,
Always on the move and so do not remember
The necessity of the silence of the islands,
The glacier floating in the distance out of existence,
The need to grip and grapple the adversary,
Knuckle on stony knuckle, to dot and carry
One and carry one and not give up the hunt
Till we have pinned the Boyg down to a point.
In England one forgets—in each performing troupe

Forgets what one has lost, there is no room to stoop
And look along the ground, one cannot see the ground
For the feet of the crowd, and the lost is never found.
I dropped something, I think, but I am not sure what
And cannot say if it mattered much or not,
So let us get on or we shall be late, for soon
The shops will close and the rush-hour be on.
This is the fret that makes us cat-like stretch
And then contract the fingers, gives the itch
To open the French window into the rain,
Walk out and never be seen at home again.
But where to go? No oracle for us,
And we like to dream of a heat which is never sultry,
Bible or Baedeker, can tell the terminus.
The songs of jazz have told us of a moon country
Melons to eat, champagne to drink, and a lazy
Music hour by hour depetalling the daisy.
Then Medici manuscripts have told of places
Where common-sense was wedded to the graces,
Doric temples and olive-trees and such,
But broken marble no longer goes for much.
And there are some who scorn this poésie de départs
And say 'Escape by staying where you are;
A man is what he thinks he is and can
Find happiness within.' How nice to be born a man.
The tourist in space or time, emotion or sensation,
Meets many guides but none have the proper orientation.
We are not changing ground to escape from facts
But rather to find them. This complex world exacts
Hard work of simplifying; to get its focus
You have to stand outside the crowd and caucus.
This all sounds somewhat priggish. You and I

92

Know very well the immediate reason why
I am in Iceland. Three months ago or so
Wystan said that he was planning to go
To Iceland to write a book—would I come too?
And I said yes, having nothing better to do.
But all the same we never make any choice
On such a merely mechanical stimulus.
The match is not the cause of fire, so pause
And look for the formal as well as the efficient cause.
Aristotle's pedantic phraseology
Serves better than common sense or hand-to-mouth
    psychology.
'ἔσχε τὴν φύσιν'—'found its nature'; the crude
Embryo rummages every latitude
Looking for itself, its nature, its final pattern,
Till the fairy godmother's wand touches the slattern
And turns her to a princess for a moment
Beyond definition or professorial comment.
We find our nature daily or try to find it,
The old flame gutters, leaves red flames behind it.
An interval of tuning and screwing and then
The symphony restarts, the creature lives again—
Blake's arabesques of fire; the subtle creature
Swings on Ezekiel's wheels, finding its nature.
In short we must keep moving to keep pace
Or else drop into Limbo, the dead place.
I have come north, gaily running away
From the grinding gears, the change from day to day,
The creaks of the familiar room, the smile
Of the cruel clock, the bills upon the file,
The excess of books and cushions, the high heels
That walk the street, the news, the newsboys' yells,

93

The flag-days and the cripple's flapping sleeve,
The ambushes of sex, the passion to retrieve
Significance from the river of passing people,
The attempt to climb the ever-climbing steeple
And no one knows what is at the top of it,
All is a raffle for caps which may not fit,
But all take tickets, keep moving; still we may
Move off from movement or change it for a day;
Here is a different rhythm, the juggled balls
Hang in the air—the pause before the soufflé falls.
Here we can take a breath, sit back, admire
Stills from the film of life, the frozen fire;
Among these rocks can roll upon the tongue
Morsels of thought, not jostled by the throng,
Or morsels of un-thought, which is still better,
(Thinking these days makes a suburban clatter).
Here we can practise forgetfulness without
A sense of guilt, fear of the tout and lout,
And here—but Wystan has butted in again
To say we must go out in the frightful rain
To see a man about a horse and so
I shall have to stop. For we soon intend to go
Around the Langjökull, a ten days' ride,
Gumboots and stockfish. Probably you'll deride
This sissy onslaught on the open spaces.
I can see the joke myself; however the case is
Not to be altered, but please remember us
So high up here in this vertiginous
Crow's-nest of the earth. Perhaps you'll let us know
If anything happens in the world below?

[1936]

94

LIFE OF LORD LEVERHULME

Lord Leverhulme was a grocer's son,
He learned to sell when he was young,
And all the tunes that he could play
Was 'Advertising makes it pay'—
    Over the hills and across the skies,
    By God it pays to advertise.

Bolton was his family seat
He rolled the shutters up in the street,
Said, 'It's time to be taking wing,'
So reorganised the book-keeping.

Travelled for his father far and wide
From Bolton round the Mersey-side
But small-scale business made him mope
So he patented the brand of Sunlight Soap.

He said, 'I must have a place to pitch,'
So he built Port Sunlight over a ditch,
And over in Europe he made his mark
Through the help of Monsieur Lavanchy-Clarke.*

Lever thought that life was sublime,
He went upstairs two at a time,
And the world saw Sunlight Soap expand,
To buy up Vinolia and Monkey Brand.

* Egyptologist and pioneer of the penny-in-the-slot machine.

Lever fought elections four
But the House of Commons had a narrow door
He saw he could try till he was dead
He would never get in for Birkenhead.

Gladstone however was Lever's pal
So he got in for Wirral as a Liberal,
And he pondered the problems by the way
Of profit sharing and the six-hour day.

Lever now made such a noise
He frightened all Lord Northcliffe's boys;
They dipped their fingers deep in mess
And libelled Lever in the daily press.

Lever promptly issued a writ,
Made fifty thousand out of it;
He said, 'I've always thought it best
To work by enlightened self-interest.'

He made his soap from vegetable oil
And said, 'I will grow what I have to boil,
My raw materials will be my own,'
So he bought large patches of the tropic zone.

Lever got up at half-past four,
Did his dozen on the bathroom floor,
Sent out orders during the day
To the Belgian Congo and the U. S. A.

Lever gave his hands a clap
And factory chimneys pimpled the map;
He had himself painted as the years wore on
By Sir William Orpen and Augustus John.

Lever said, 'All good business men
Should read the Book of Proverbs now and then';
He sailed the Niger black as night
And he left his name on a jungle site.

Lever smiled and stepped on the gas,
He said, 'My life will be no impasse,
Just you watch the speedo climb—
I'm getting somewhere all the time.'

Nearing seventy Lever said,
'Just one more coup before I'm dead:
I'll help those lame dogs over their stiles,
I'll stamp my name on the Western Isles.'

He bought up Lewis and then he began
To chart and build and kipper and can;
Every item was to run to scheme,
There'd be no hitches in the new régime.

He took the roof off over his bed
And he founded MacFisheries Limited
That the British householder might get
His northern herring fresh from the net.

Lever said, 'What a charming clime,'
He went up the stairs two at a time;
He said, 'It's hard but before I'm done
I'll give the Lews a place in the sun.'

But Lever's totalitarian plan
Was caviare to the Lewisman;
Our lands, they said, to us belong
And they raided the farms at Gress and Tong.

Lever said that he was afraid
The men of Lewis were retrograde,
He wrote to the Minister of Scottish Affairs
And said, 'This island needs repairs.

I'd hand them happiness on a plate
If only the fools would co-operate
But blind with Celtic mist and phlegm
They cannot see what is good for them.'

The Scottish minister held his hand
And the raiders squatted on Lever's land,
They said, 'This Saxon Lord of the Isles
Can go somewhere else to make his piles.'

He rode round Lewis in a powerful car
And he saw that progress was anathema;
He said, 'There's nothing more I can do,
The Isle of Lewis is my Waterloo.'

He called the people together one day
And he gave them the Parish of Stornoway
And the rest of Lewis he sold in blocks
To people who wanted a shooting box

To the Island of Harris he turned his eyes
As more adapted to enterprise;
He introduced his commercial cult—
Leverburgh is the sole result.

Leverburgh was meant to be
The hub of the fishing industry;
All that remained at Lever's death
Was a waste of money and a waste of breath.

All that remained of Lever's plans
Were some half-built piers and some empty cans,
And the islanders with no regrets
Treated each other to cigarettes.

Lever started the heavenly climb,
He went up the stairs two at a time.
St. Peter said, 'Make room, make room,
Here comes Viscount Leverhulme.'

St. Peter said, 'Don't be cross with me
But this is a mere formality;
Have you any *failure* to confess?'
And Lever truthfully answered, 'Yes.

All through my life I've made my bit
From my day of birth to my obiit
And all my life I've done my best
In the cause of Enlightened Self-interest.

I asked for nothing but a little rope
And I paved Piccadilly with Sunlight Soap.
Organisation was my flair—
Organisation and savoir faire.

In any deed that I had to do
The thought of failure was taboo,
Only once in time till now
Did I take my hand from off the plough.

I left my programme incomplete,
The Western Islands had me beat.'
St. Peter said, 'I'm not surprised;
To tackle Lewis was ill-advised.

The Scottish Islands are a rotten deal,
Those Celts are terribly *difficile;*
We find them unwilling to pull their weight
When we let them in at the Golden Gate.

They've no team spirit, they won't take part
In our study circles and community art
And at garden parties they won't concur
In speaking English—which is *de rigueur.*

No one here will consider it
The least reflection on your native wit
That the ignorant crofters, penny-wise,
Should have sabotaged your enterprise.

So welcome now to the realms divine
And sign your name on the dotted line.
You'll find the life up here a spree
For Heaven is a joint-stock company.'

Lever signed on the dotted line
And took one look at the realms divine;
He said, 'The streets are gold but why
Are there no sky-signs in the sky?'

Next day he rose at half-past four,
Pitched his desk on the golden floor.
He said, 'Where there aren't any seas
There can't be any Hebrides.'

Lever looked up from his heavenly files,
Said, 'The devil may take those Western Isles.
In Heaven now is all my hope
And I'll sell the angels Sunlight Soap.

100

They keep this place too blessed dark,
Send me up M. Lavanchy-Clarke;
The blest will open their blessed eyes
When they see what it means to advertise.'

He began the business then and there
And the stocks in Heaven rose like air;
The Devil's business fell as flat
As a nudist camp or an opera hat.

But far below in the Western Seas
The moors were quiet in the Hebrides,
The crofters gossiped in Gaelic speech
And the waves crept over the lonely beach.

[1937]

THE HEBRIDES

On those islands
The west wind drops its messages of indolence,
No one hurries, the Gulf Stream warms the gnarled
Rampart of gneiss, the feet of the peasant years
Pad up and down their sentry-beat not challenging
Any comer for the password—only Death
Comes through unchallenged in his general's cape.
The houses straggle on the umber moors,
The Aladdin lamp mutters in the boarded room
Where a woman smoors the fire of fragrant peat.
No one repeats the password for it is known,
All is known before it comes to the lips—
Instinctive wisdom. Over the fancy vases

101

The photos with the wrinkles taken out,
The enlarged portraits of the successful sons
Who married wealth in Toronto or New York,
Console the lonely evenings of the old
Who live embanked by memories of labour
And child-bearing and scriptural commentaries.
On those islands
The boys go poaching their ancestral rights—
The Ossianic salmon who take the yellow
Tilt of the river with a magnet's purpose—
And listen breathless to the tales at the ceilidh
Among the peat-smoke and the smells of dung
That fill the felted room from the cave of the byre.
No window opens of the windows sunk like eyes
In a four-foot wall of stones casually picked
From the knuckly hills on which these houses crawl
Like black and legless beasts who breathe in their sleep
Among the piles of peat and pooks of hay—
A brave oasis in the indifferent moors.
And while the stories circulate like smoke,
The sense of life spreads out from the one-eyed house
In wider circles through the lake of night
In which articulate man has dropped a stone—
In wider circles round the black-faced sheep,
Wider and fainter till they hardly crease
The ebony heritage of the herded dead.
On those islands
The tinkers whom no decent girl will go with,
Preserve the Gaelic tunes unspoiled by contact
With the folk-fancier or the friendly tourist,
And preserve the knowledge of horse-flesh and preserve
The uncompromising empire of the rogue.

On those islands
The tethered cow grazes among the orchises
And figures in blue calico turn by hand
The ground beyond the plough, and the bus, not stop-
     ping,
Drops a parcel for the lonely household
Where men remembering stories of eviction
Are glad to have their land though mainly stones—
The honoured bones which still can hoist a body.
On those islands
There is echo of the leaping fish, the identical
Sound that cheered the chiefs at ease from slaughter;
There is echo of baying hounds of a lost breed
And echo of MacCrimmon's pipes lost in the cave;
And seals cry with the voices of the drowned.
When men go out to fish, no one must say 'Good luck'
And the confidences told in a boat at sea
Must be as if printed on the white ribbon of a wave
Withdrawn as soon as printed—so never heard.
On those islands
The black minister paints the tour of hell
While the unregenerate drink from the bottle's neck
In gulps like gauntlets thrown at the devil's head
And spread their traditional songs across the hills
Like fraying tapestries of fights and loves,
The boar-hunt and the rope let down at night—
Lost causes and lingering home-sickness.
On those islands
The fish come singing from the drunken sea,
The herring rush the gunwales and sort themselves
To cram the expectant barrels of their own accord—
Or such is the dream of the fisherman whose wet

Leggings hang on the door as he sleeps returned
From a night when miles of net were drawn up empty.
On those islands
A girl with candid eyes goes out to marry
An independent tenant of seven acres
Who goes each year to the south to work on the roads
In order to raise a rent of forty shillings,
And all the neighbours celebrate their wedding
With drink and pipes and the walls of the barn reflect
The crazy shadows of the whooping dancers.
On those islands
Where many live on the dole or on old-age pensions
And many waste with consumption and some are
        drowned
And some of the old stumble in the midst of sleep
Into the pot-hole hitherto shunned in dreams
Or falling from the cliff among the shrieks of gulls
Reach the bottom before they have time to wake—
Whoever dies on the islands and however
The whole of the village goes into three-day mourning,
The afflicted home is honoured and the shops are shut
For on those islands
Where a few surnames cover a host of people
And the art of being a stranger with your neighbour
Has still to be imported, death is still
No lottery ticket in a public lottery—
The result to be read on the front page of a journal—
But a family matter near to the whole family.
On those islands
Where no train runs on rails and the tyrant time
Has no clock-towers to signal people to doom
With semaphore ultimatums tick by tick,

There is still peace though not for me and not
Perhaps for long—still peace on the bevel hills
For those who still can live as their fathers lived
On those islands.

[1937]

IV

OUT OF THE PICTURE: 1936–1937

[Excerpts from a play]

THE ORACLE

The oracle
  High between the cliffs,
The tripod over
  The mephitic cleft,
Or the sybil's cave
  Where the winds blow
The dead leaf answers
  To and fro:
Where shall we find truth in an oracle?

The oracle
  Among the talking oaks,
The flight of birds,
  The examination of guts,
Luck of the cards,
  Lines of the hand,
Call of the raven
  In a sallow land:
Where shall we find truth in an oracle?

THE DAILY NEWS

The news that blows around the streets
Or vibrates over the air
Whether it is rape, embezzlement or murder
Seems frivolous, if not farcical, without dignity.
Whereas the actual fact before it becomes news
Is often tragic even when commonplace.
The daily press gives neither laughter nor tears

But the stage of life gives both.
We wish to remind you that upon this stage
Slapstick may turn to swordplay,
The cottage flowers may give a sudden hiss
The trees curve down their hands in heavy gloves—
A malediction on the nape of the neck.
We will tell you a little fable:
There was a picnic party in the eighteenth century
Strayed out of canvas with their lutes and beakers
And called among the rocks to the lady Echo
But Echo missed her cue
And instead of returning the same coin they gave her,
Phrases of music and gallant phrases,
Echo like a gorgon glared from the sudden rocks
And cried in a stony voice the one word 'Death.'
These possibilities should always be remembered
But for the moment let us go back to our farce.

RIDING IN CARS

Riding in cars
    On tilting roads
We have left behind
    Our household gods,
We have left behind
    The cautious clause,
The laws of the over-
    rational mind.

Frost on the window,
    Skaters' figures,
110

Gunmen fingering
    Anxious triggers,
Stocks and shares
    (The ribbon of the rich),
The favourite down
    At the blind ditch.

Forgotten now
    The early days,
Youth's idyllic
    And dawdling ways;
Cruising along
    On the long road
We do not notice
    The limping god.

Swinging between
    Crutches he comes
To an overture
    Of buried drums;
His eyes will turn
    Our hands to stone,
His name is Time,
    He walks alone.

HYMN OF THE COLLECTORS

Spring comes with drums and jonquils
    And smells of French fern soap
And telephones keep ringing
    Insistent bells of hope;

Some gather New Year honours
    Enrolled as knight or bart
And some like us pay homage
    Before the shrines of Art.

Then gather all ye faithful
    Combined against the foe,
The philistine and film-fan,
    The bitch, the hog, the crow.
They snuffle in their nosebags,
    They drag the hangman's cart
But we will hold our noses
    And cull the fruits of Art.

So gather in this precinct
    Before the days grow worse
With reverence on your eyelids
    And money in your purse;
And since the cheque for thousands
    Reveals the contrite heart
Bid high the fancy prices
    Of priceless works of Art.

WAR HEROES

When the heroes came back from the ten years' war
(But no war now will last ten years)
They struck a port they seemed to have seen before.
There were old men sitting on the bollards
Puffing smoke across the sea,
There were dead men hanging in the gantries,

There was a lame bird limping on the quay.
When were we here before? one of them said.
The captain answered: This is where we were born
And where we have now returned. Dead to the Dead.

PINDAR IS DEAD

There are hikers on all the roads—
  Pindar is dead—
The petrol pumps are doing a roaring business,
Motors are tuning up for the Easter races,
Building companies are loaning to the newly married—
  Pindar is dead and that's no matter.

There are climbers on all the hills—
  Pindar is dead—
With oiled boots and ropes they are tackling Snowdon,
The swimming-baths are filled for Easter Monday,
Doctored with chlorine to prevent infection—
  Pindar is dead and that's no matter.

There is money on all the horses—
  Pindar is dead—
One belongs to a proud and a plethoric peer,
One to a maharajah, one to a midland magnate,
One to a dago count and one to a tweeded spinster—
  Pindar is dead and that's no matter.

There are flowers in all the markets—
  Pindar is dead—

Daffodils, tulips, and forced roses,
New potatoes and green peas for Easter,
Wreaths of moss and primrose for the churches
But no wreaths for runners, whether of olive or laurel—
  Pindar is dead and that's no matter.

LES NEIGES D'ANTAN

What's become of all the glory and the grandeur of the
    gold-men and the gunmen,
The long breakers topped with silver of expanding power
    and profits,
Of the well-upholstered mansion, seven flights of stairs
    for the servants
Carrying coal from six in the morning?
What's become of the squadron of butlers, valets, grooms
    and second housemaids?
Gone like the carriage-horse and cabhorse that once
    dunged the streets of London.
What's become of the oracles in beards and whiskers,
    beauty in bustles?
What's become of Mr. Gladstone or of Grandpa's roll-top
    desk,
Waterloo Bridge and General Gordon?
What's become of them? What's becoming of us?
Look ahead, Long-Sighted Jim,
What do you see in the future dim?
  I look ahead and what do I see?
  I see a pageant, a Lord Mayor's procession,
  The Aldermen and the flunkeys, the carnival giants,
  The tableaux on lorries, the flags and the coaches,

And every single one of the people who make that
     procession
Carries a white stick to show that he is blind.
What's become of the light of day, the golden spokes of
     the sun's wheels,
What's become of the fingers of light that picked the
     locks of the dark places,
What's become of all our private sentinels?
     Answer: The sentry has gone.
     He will not come back.
     The pavement was worn by his feet
     But moss will grow over the tracks.
     Anyone now can approach
     The door of your house without fear.
     The burglar, the beggar, the drunk,
     The murdering madman, the whore,
     The prophet in sackcloth, the priest,
     The jackal, the tiger, the snake,
     All have their eye on your door.

Chorus

Close all the doors, bar all the shutters,
Be ready with revolver and electric torch,
Fire extinguisher and telephone directory,
Bible, cheque book and *savoir faire:*
The vultures are gathered together,
Their hooked wings carve the urban air.
When the golden cycle is over, the wise men said,
Fire will consume the lot, the game resume,
And feathers of the birds of prey will singe as they tear
     the prey,

And the corpses roast where they fell
And the small blue flames will play
Like kittens with a ball of wool . . .
       FIRE   FIRE   FIRE   FIRE . . .
Fire in Troy, fire in Babylon, fire in Nineveh, fire in
    London,
       FIRE   FIRE   FIRE   FIRE
The buckets are empty of water, the hoses are punctured,
The city main is cut off, the holy well is dry,
There is no succour in the dusty ground, the metallic sky,
No rock will spout with water at the prophet's rod,
Nor fate repeat the legendary flood,
There is nothing to stem the mechanical march of fire,
Nothing to assuage the malice of the drunken fire.
       FIRE   FIRE   FIRE   FIRE

EMPTY SHOES

Some one said that shoes had personality,
That when you die your shoes . . .
That the frozen overflow of personality
Hangs on in jags after the general thaw
When a man has died.
Icicles, acroteria.
In a corner, in a cloakroom, among rackets and rods
An old pair of brogues
With criss-cross wrinkles like an old man's face.
Or when a girl has died
Her shoes are lined up, spruce as soldiers,
Waiting for the word Dismiss.

And in hotels at night passing from door to door
There is something terrible in all those empty shoes.
Frozen overflow of personality . . .

ANNOUNCER'S SONG

We're out of the picture,
  Out of the picture.
Once we made a song and dance
Every man his own free lance
Every girl a Circe or
A Helen on a golden floor,
Once we held the pose—and how!
  But now
We're out of the picture,
  Out of the picture now.

We're out of the picture,
  Out of the picture.
No more we comb our auburn locks
Among the Quattrocento rocks
And stand as harlequin no more
Upon the grey nostalgic shore,
Once we graced a galleon's prow
  But now
We're out of the picture,
  Out of the picture now.

We're out of the picture,
  Out of the picture.
Not free to wear the bishop's gown,

The hero's belt, the martyr's crown,
Not rich enough to keep the tone
Nor call our bloody souls our own,
No private niche these times allow
   For now
We're out of the picture,
   Out of the picture now.

We're out of the picture,
   Out of the picture.
The foreground needs men in the mass
Beneath a sky of bombs and gas;
The daily grind, the common street
Dethrone, disown the old élite.
Our carriage founders in the slough
   For now
We're out of the picture,
   Out of the picture now.

VENUS' SPEECH

So you think it is all a matter of love?
And what do you think love is a matter of?
Matter is the word for it.
Atoms—permutations, combinations of atoms.
It's not just a fancy ballet, a *fête champêtre*.
The cycle of life demands to be repeated.
You were made by your parents, you must make in re-
   turn,
You must make children for Death.
Death is a sculptor, you must quarry him marble,

His chisel will find the shape in the blind block.
What you call love is merely an incident;
Wait till you see the end of it.
There is a city beyond this life, no flesh or blood there,
No food in the shops, no fire in the grates, no smoke from
the chimneys;
All the people that have ever lived walk there
Renouncing their living,
All the people that have ever loved walk there
Renouncing their loving,
But they do not even think this renunciation
For their brains are solid, of stone,
Their heads and their eyes are of stone,
Being no longer organisms of nature
But final versions of an artist's vision.
For the art of man is supererogation;
Man himself will be a work of art in the end.
Man should not emulate the artist, Death.
Let not man be contriving a frozen beauty;
While he is here and now let him deal in here and now,
Work and fight for meat and love,
Gallant approximation, bravado of defeat.
I am the principle of Unity and Division,
Multiplication by pain,
Spawning of worlds from a discord
Always recurring,
I am the attempt to cover the abyss with grass
And to spangle the grass with flowers
And to put there cattle grazing the grass
And young men picking the flowers,
And to make believe through elaboration of pattern
That life goes on for ever.

Which, thanks to me, is true in a sense.
Which, thanks to me, is true in the world of sense
Though it is not true in the world of precise death,
The world of pure idea, mating statues.
Go to your work, children, the tide is coming in,
The strip of sand is narrow,
You have not much time if you wish to get married,
You have not much time if you wish to build castles.
Blessed are the reckless spendthrifts of vitality
But blessed also are all who last the course,
Blessed are those who endure as a point of etiquette
And blessed are the cynics who carry their cross as a
    gesture.
Do you remember when you were six years old
The text in the parish church at Christmas,
'Peace on Earth, Goodwill to Men,'
And Christ's lips moving in the stained glass window;
There were no lipreaders present
But I can tell you what he said.
'I come bringing not peace,' he said. 'I come
Bringing not peace but a sword.'
All to their posts. The drum is beating.
Diver, descend. Ploughman, drive your team.
Grapple the bulk of the sea, challenge the flinty soil;
The furrows are there in advance as music is there in
    the air
Waiting to be realised upon the fiddler's bow.

CHORUS

Sleep and wake, sleep and wake,
Sleep to wake but wake to sleep,
120

And body calling body make
A further body, the insistent task
Of rolling a stone up the steep
Hill of hell, of rolling a stone
Away from the tomb and do not ask
Who comes forth in the dawn alone.

THE JINGLES OF THE MORNING

Shall we remember the jingles of the morning,
The pipers the pedlars and the brass farthings,
The buds of music, the imagined darlings?
   No, we shall *not* remember.

Shall we remember the games with puffball and plantain,
Searching for the lost handle to the silent fountain,
Hiding in the shrubbery, shutting our eyes and counting?

Shall we remember the marigolds parading,
Smell of grass and noise of the corncrake railing
And the fun of dragging a stick along the paling?

And after that shall we remember the races,
The broken tape, the clamour of companions' voices,
The schoolboy's callow joys in smut and curses?

And shall we remember our early adult pleasure,
The dive in love's lagoons of brilliant azure,
The gay martyrdom, the brave fantasia.

Shall we remember the kick of inspired religion,
The visions in drink, the feel of the homing pigeon
Drawn by a magnet to an intuited region?

Shall we remember the noise of the moving nations
Or shall we remember the gusty sun's creations,
The night and the never-to-be-climbed-to constellations?
  No, we shall *not* remember.

AUCTIONEER'S SPEECH

One two three four.
One two three four.
Can you turn these stones to bread?
Any offers for a loaf of bread?
Any offers for a sinking world?
One two three four,
One two three four.
Any offers, ladies and gentlemen?
Any offers, comrades?
Any offers, any offers, for a last look at the peep-show,
A seat in the back of the pit at the last performance?
Think of the good old times and buy a ticket for charity—
Should auld acquaintance be forgot—
Think of the humdrum comfort of your cherished lives
Safe in the morning train behind perspiring windows
And in the evening train crumpling the evening paper
Between the dirty green of soccer-fields and the shining
Suburban cemetery and the smoky trees
Brimming in twilight with the sparrows' palaver;
Even then you thought you were dragooned to duty,

To dot and carry one and carry one,
Carry the cross whose arms stretch out to heaven
Hung with the vermin of minutes, rat and stoat.
One two three four,
One two three four.
The show is closing; is there not a single offer?
If not for love, from a sense of martyred pride?
Was it not good after all to have once been born
And have said to yourself 'This is nobody else but I
And the world about me is mine and therefore good—
My world, my mother and mistress, to be fought,
Gained and regained and moulded to my mind,
Ravished from virgin silence, forced to speak
The answer which I felt but could not frame?'
For that world, living still but at such odds
As no insurance company would take,
Who makes a bid, my friends, who makes a bid?
Who gambles on this bird with the broken wing,
This missing engine, this cracked bell, this heap
Of scuttering ants beneath the great beast's foot?
It is your last chance which is here and now—
The naked legs of children laced with foam,
Waving their spades around a tower of sand—
It is going, going, among the flux of words,
Three thousand years of a wordy civilisation,
Tags and slogans, nursery rhymes and prayers
Resolved at last to a drowning gasp for breath.
Our world is going, going—going for a song,
Going for a next to nothing, a nought, a cypher,
Going for the winning time of last year's athletes,
Going for a wisp of paper, a wraith of power,
A cripple's dream of life as a steeple-jack

Or the odds on driving back the one-way street
That leads to death, going for a moment more,
For a last minute speculation on Why and Who—
Who above all it was whom once we loved,
Whose face we cannot remember but whose hands
We still can feel in the dark like a man in a boat
Dangling his hand in the water flowing and going
Going for ever under collapsing bridges
Going going—going through veils of mist
Through walls of air, through gates of glassy music
Striated dark and never-guessed-at corners.
And over an edge and down a ramp of light
One two three four,
One two three four.
GOING   GOING   GOING   GONE

FINALE

It is not enough
To have winning ways,
    The trimmed wick burns clear,
To follow with an indolent eye
The flicker-pattern of the days,
    For here ends our hoarded oil.

The acquisitive arts
Are not enough,
    The trimmed wick burns clear,
It is a little and a tired time
To be making money or love,
    Here ends our hoarded oil.

A kiss, a cuddle,
A crossed cheque,
  The trimmed wick burns clear,
Walk among statues in the dark,
The odds are you will break your neck—
  Here ends our hoarded oil.

V

POEMS: 1936–1938

CARRICKFERGUS

I was born in Belfast between the mountain and the
     gantries
   To the hooting of lost sirens and the clang of trams:
Thence to Smoky Carrick in County Antrim
   Where the bottle-neck harbour collects the mud which
     jams

The little boats beneath the Norman castle,
   The pier shining with lumps of crystal salt;
The Scotch Quarter was a line of residential houses
   But the Irish Quarter was a slum for the blind and halt.

The brook ran yellow from the factory stinking of
     chlorine,
   The yarn-mill called its funeral cry at noon;
Our lights looked over the lough to the lights of Bangor
   Under the peacock aura of a drowning moon.

The Norman walled this town against the country
   To stop his ears to the yelping of his slave
And built a church in the form of a cross but denoting
   The list of Christ on the cross, in the angle of the nave.

I was the rector's son, born to the anglican order,
   Banned for ever from the candles of the Irish poor;
The Chichesters knelt in marble at the end of a transept
   With ruffs about their necks, their portion sure.

The war came and a huge camp of soldiers
   Grew from the ground in sight of our house with long

Dummies hanging from gibbets for bayonet practice
　　And the sentry's challenge echoing all day long;

A Yorkshire terrier ran in and out by the gate-lodge
　　Barred to civilians, yapping as if taking affront:
Marching at ease and singing 'Who Killed Cock Robin?'
　　The troops went out by the lodge and off to the Front.

The steamer was camouflaged that took me to England—
　　Sweat and khaki in the Carlisle train;
I thought that the war would last for ever and sugar
　　Be always rationed and that never again

Would the weekly papers not have photos of sandbags
　　And my governess not make bandages from moss
And people not have maps above the fireplace
　　With flags on pins moving across and across—

Across the hawthorn hedge the noise of bugles,
　　Flares across the night,
Somewhere on the lough was a prison ship for Germans,
　　A cage across their sight.

I went to school in Dorset, the world of parents
　　Contracted into a puppet world of sons
Far from the mill girls, the smell of porter, the salt-mines
　　And the soldiers with their guns.

　　　　　　　　　　　　　　　　　[1937]

PASSAGE STEAMER

Upon the decks they take beef tea
　　Who are so free, so free, so free,
But down the ladder in the engine-room
　　(Doom, doom, doom, doom)
The great cranks rise and fall, repeat,
The great cranks plod with their Assyrian feet
　　To match the monotonous energy of the sea.

Back from a journey I require
　　Some new desire, desire, desire
But find in the open sea and sun
　　None, none, none, none;
The gulls that bank around the mast
Insinuate that nothing we pass is past,
　　That all our beginnings were long since begun.

And when I think of you, my dear,
　　Who were so near, so near, so near,
The barren skies from wall to wall
　　Appal, appal, pall, pall,
The spray no longer gilds the wave,
The sea looks nothing more nor less than a grave
　　And the world and the day are grey and that is all.
　　　　　　　　　　　　　　　　　　[1936]

NOCTURNE

Now that the shapes of mist like hooded beggar-children
Slink quickly along the middle of the road
And the lamps draw trails of milk in ponds of lustrous
    lead
I am decidedly pleased not to be dead.

Or when wet roads at night reflect the clutching
Importunate fingers of trees and windy shadows
Lunge and flounce on the windshield as I drive
I am glad of the accident of being alive.

There are so many nights with stars or close-
ly interleaved with battleship-grey or plum,
So many visitors whose Buddha-like palms are pressed
Against the windowpanes where people take their rest.

Whose favour now is yours to screen your sleep—
You need not hear the strings that are tuning for the
    dawn—
Mingling, my dear, your breath with the quiet breath
Of Sleep whom the old writers called the brother of
    Death.

[1936]

ICELAND

No shields now
   Cross the knoll,
The hills are dull
   With leaden shale,

Whose arms could squeeze
  The breath from time
And the climb is long
  From cairn to cairn.

Houses are few
  But decorous
In a ruined land
  Of sphagnum moss;
Corrugated iron
  Farms inherit
The spirit and phrase
  Of ancient sagas.

Men have forgotten
  Anger and ambush,
To make ends meet
  Their only business:
The lover riding
  In the lonely dale
Hears the plover's
  Single pipe

And feels perhaps
  But undefined
The drift of death
  In the sombre wind
Deflating the trim
  Balloon of lust
In a grey storm
  Of dust and grit.

So we who have come
  As trippers North
Have minds no match
  For this land's girth;
The glacier's licking
  Tongues deride
Our pride of life,
  Our flashy songs.

But the people themselves
  Who live here
Ignore the brooding
  Fear, the sphinx;
And the radio
  With tags of tune
Defies their pillared
  Basalt crags.

Whose ancestors
  Thought that at last
The end would come
  To a blast of horns
And gods would face
  The worst in fight,
Vanish in the night
  The last, the first

Night which began
  Without device
In ice and rocks,
  No shade or shape;

134

Grass and blood,
   The strife of life,
Were an interlude
   Which soon must pass

And all go back
   Relapse to rock
Under the shawl
   Of the ice-caps,
The cape which night
   Will spread to cover
The world when the living
   Flags are furled.

                                [1936]

EPILOGUE TO ICELAND

For W. H. Auden

Now the winter nights begin
Lonely comfort walls me in;
So before the memory slip
I review our Iceland trip—

Not for me romantic nor
Idyll on a mythic shore
But a fancy turn, you know,
Sandwiched in a graver show.

Down in Europe Seville fell,
Nations germinating hell,
The Olympic games were run—
Spots upon the Aryan sun.

135

And the don in me set forth
How the landscape of the north
Had educed the saga style
Plodding forward mile by mile.

And the don in you replied
That the North begins inside,
Our ascetic guts require
Breathers from the Latin fire.

So although no ghost was scotched
We were happy while we watched
Ravens from their walls of shale
Cruise around the rotting whale,

Watched the sulphur basins boil,
Loops of steam uncoil and coil,
While the valley fades away
To a sketch of Judgment Day.

So we rode and joked and smoked
With no miracles evoked,
With no levitations won
In the thin unreal sun;

In that island never found
Visions blossom from the ground,
No conversions like St. Paul,
No great happenings at all.

Holidays should be like this,
Free from over-emphasis,
Time for soul to stretch and spit
Before the world comes back on it,

Before the chimneys row on row
Sneer in smoke, 'We told you so'
And the fog-bound sirens call
Ruin to the long sea-wall.

Rows of books around me stand,
Fence me round on either hand;
Through that forest of dead words
I would hunt the living birds—

Great black birds that fly alone
Slowly through a land of stone,
And the gulls who weave a free
Quilt of rhythm on the sea.

Here in Hampstead I sit late
Nights which no one shares and wait
For the phone to ring or for
Unknown angels at the door;

Better were the northern skies
Than this desert in disguise—
Rugs and cushions and the long
Mirror which repeats the song.

For the litany of doubt
From these walls comes breathing out
Till the room becomes a pit
Humming with the fear of it

With the fear of loneliness
And uncommunicableness;
All the wires are cut, my friends
Live beyond the severed ends.

So I write these lines for you
Who have felt the death-wish too,
But your lust for life prevails—
Drinking coffee, telling tales.

Our prerogatives as men
Will be cancelled who knows when;
Still I drink your health before
The gun-butt raps upon the door.

[1936]

SOLVITUR ACRIS HIEMS

(Horace, Odes, I. 4)

Winter to Spring: the west wind melts the frozen rancour,
    The windlass drags to sea the thirsty hull;
Byre is no longer welcome to beast or fire to ploughman,
    The field removes the frost-cap from his skull.

Venus of Cythera leads the dances under the hanging
    Moon and the linked line of Nymphs and Graces
Beat the ground with measured feet while the busy Fire-
        God
    Stokes his red-hot mills in volcanic places.

Now is the time to twine the spruce and shining head
        with myrtle,
    Now with flowers escaped the earthy fetter,
And sacrifice to the woodland god in shady copses
    A lamb or a kid, whichever he likes better.

138

Equally heavy is the heel of white-faced Death on the
          pauper's
     Shack and the towers of kings, and O my dear
The little sum of life forbids the ravelling of lengthy
     Hopes. Night and the fabled dead are near

And the narrow house of nothing past whose lintel
     You will meet no wine like this, no boy to admire
Like Lycidas who to-day makes all young men a furnace
     And whom to-morrow girls will find a fire.

                                        [1937]

THE SUNLIGHT ON THE GARDEN

          The sunlight on the garden
          Hardens and grows cold,
          We cannot cage the minute
          Within its nets of gold;
          When all is told
          We cannot beg for pardon.

          Our freedom as free lances
          Advances towards its end;
          The earth compels, upon it
          Sonnets and birds descend;
          And soon, my friend,
          We shall have no time for dances.

          The sky was good for flying
          Defying the church bells
          And every evil iron
                    139

Siren and what it tells:
The earth compels,
We are dying, Egypt, dying

And not expecting pardon,
Hardened in heart anew,
But glad to have sat under
Thunder and rain with you,
And grateful too
For sunlight on the garden.

[1937]

JUNE THUNDER

The Junes were free and full, driving through tiny
Roads, the mudguards brushing the cowparsley,
Through fields of mustard and under boldly embattled
     Mays and chestnuts

Or between beeches verdurous and voluptuous
Or where broom and gorse beflagged the chalkland—
All the flare and gusto of the unenduring
     Joys of a season

Now returned but I note as more appropriate
To the maturer moods impending thunder
With an indigo sky and the garden hushed except for
     The treetops moving.

Then the curtains in my room blow suddenly inward,
The shrubbery rustles, birds fly heavily homeward,

140

The white flowers fade to nothing on the trees and rain
          comes
      Down like a dropscene.

Now there comes the catharsis, the cleansing downpour
Breaking the blossoms of our overdated fancies
Our old sentimentality and whimsicality
      Loves of the morning.

Blackness at half-past eight, the night's precursor,
Clouds like falling masonry and lightning's lavish
Annunciation, the sword of the mad archangel
      Flashed from the scabbard.

If only now you would come and dare the crystal
Rampart of rain and the bottomless moat of thunder,
If only now you would come I should be happy
      Now if now only.

                          [1937]

THE HEATED MINUTES

The heated minutes climb
The anxious hill,
The tills fill up with cash,
The tiny hammers chime
The bells of good and ill,
And the world piles with ash
From fingers killing time.

If you were only here
Among these rocks,
I should not feel the dull
The taut and ticking fear
That hides in all the clocks
And creeps inside the skull—
If you were here, my dear.

[1937]

LEAVING BARRA

The dazzle on the sea, my darling,
Leads from the western channel
A carpet of brilliance taking
My leave for ever of the island.

I never shall visit that island
Again with its easy tempo—
The seal sunbathing, the circuit
Of gulls on the wing for garbage.

I go to a different garbage
And scuffle for scraps of notice,
Pretend to ignore the stigma
That stains my life and my leisure.

For fretful even in leisure
I fidget for different values,
Restless as a gull and haunted
By a hankering after Atlantis.

I do not know that Atlantis
Unseen and uncomprehended,
Dimly divined but keenly
Felt with a phantom hunger.

If only I could crush the hunger
If only I could lay the phantom
Then I should no doubt be happy
Like a fool or a dog or a buddha.

O the self-abnegation of Buddha
The belief that is disbelieving
The denial of chiaroscuro
Not giving a damn for existence!

But I would cherish existence
Loving the beast and the bubble
Loving the rain and the rainbow,
Considering philosophy alien.

For all the religions are alien
That allege that life is a fiction,
And when we agree in denial
The cock crows in the morning.

If only I could wake in the morning
And find I had learned the solution,
Wake with the knack of knowledge
Who as yet have only an inkling.

Though some facts foster the inkling—
The beauty of the moon and music,
The routine courage of the worker,
The gay endurance of women,

And you who to me among women
Stand for so much that I wish for,
I thank you, my dear, for the example
Of living in tune and moving.

For few are able to keep moving,
They drag and flag in the traffic;
While you are alive beyond question
Like the dazzle on the sea, my darling.

[1937]

SAND IN THE AIR

Books, do not look at me,
    Clock, do not stare;
The fire's ashes fidget,
    There is sand in the air;
Drums tell its coming—
    The sandstorm that blows
From the desert of darkness—
    O in the desert of darkness
        Where is she walking?

Otherwise regular
    Quickening their beat
The marchers of madness
    Pick up their feet,
Make for my table
    And the empty chair
That faces me—Where,
    Where and why is she absent
        Leaving it empty?

144

Dial her number,
　　None will reply;
In the shrivelled world
　　There is only I;
Her voice is frozen,
　　Hangs in my brain
On the crags of memory—
　　O my dear, go away
　　　From the crags of memory.

　　　　　　　　　　　　　　[1936]

DEPARTURE PLATFORM

Love, my love, it is high time to travel,
　　The brass bell clangs escape
And summer in a porter's cap will punch our tickets
　　And launch us where the shining lines unravel.

We have been there before though we have not seen it—
　　The land that was always ours
Whose stones are our bones', whose rivers our blood's
　　　　kindred,
　　A land without a meaning unless we mean it.

The distance opens like a mouth to meet us
　　Wantonly tongue to tongue
Consummating our dreams by night, defeating
　　The daily thoughts which day by day defeat us.

Divined but never known—the evasive universal;
　　For, fumbling after the scent

Dissolved in the running water of time we fool our fancy
  To catch intact what is always in dispersal.

And on this quest in company with many
  We hoard our hopes a year
To blow in a fortnight—a dandelion puffball
  Telling the past time and the spent penny.

So pack like the others, be sure you look your best for
  This year's unlikely chance;
Whether it is France or Wales or the Canary Islands
  The place—who knows—is a person to be well-dressed
    for.

Unlikely; and, were that so, I should be jealous
  Unless that god of the place
Could fuse his person with mine for your enjoyment—
  But whether he could there is nobody can tell us.

But on the off chance pack—your summer frocks and
    sandals
  And a pair of gloves for towns
And one small bottle of scent—Chanel or Coty—
  And your long ear-rings twisted like Christmas candles.

It leaves at three-fifteen—with lifting pistons—
  The zero hour;
Opposite in corner seats we hope for nearness
  And dearness in what is wrongly called the distance.
                                                    [1938]

TRILOGY FOR X

I

When clerks and navvies fondle
  Beside canals their wenches,
In rapture or in coma
  The haunches that they handle,
And the orange moon sits idle
  Above the orchard slanted—
Upon such easy evenings
  We take our loves for granted.

But when, as now, the creaking
  Trees on the hills of London
Like bison charge their neighbours
  In wind that keeps us waking
And in the draught the scolloped
  Lampshade swings a shadow,
We think of love bound over—
  The mortgage on the meadow.

And one lies lonely, haunted
  By limbs he half remembers,
And one, in wedlock, wonders
  Where is the girl he wanted;
And some sit smoking, flicking
  The ash away and feeling
For love gone up like vapour
  Between the floor and ceiling.

But now when winds are curling
    The trees do you come closer,
Close as an eyelid fasten
    My body in darkness, darling;
Switch the light off and let me
    Gather you up and gather
The power of trains advancing
    Further, advancing further.

II

And love hung still as crystal over the bed
    And filled the corners of the enormous room;
The boom of dawn that left her sleeping, showing
    The flowers mirrored in the mahogany table.

O my love, if only I were able
    To protract this hour of quiet after passion,
Not ration happiness but keep this door for ever
    Closed on the world, its own world closed within it.

But dawn's waves trouble with the bubbling minute,
    The names of books come clear upon their shelves,
The reason delves for duty and you will wake
    With a start and go on living on your own.

The first train passes and the windows groan,
    Voices will hector and your voice become
A drum in tune with theirs, which all last night
    Like sap that fingered through a hungry tree
Asserted our one night's identity.

III

March gave clear days,
  Gave unaccustomed sunshine,
Prelude to who knows
  What dead end or downfall;
O my love, to
  Browse in the painted prelude.

Regent's Park was
  Gay with ducks and deck-chairs,
Omens were absent,
  Cooks bought cloves and parsley;
O my love, to
  Stop one's ear to omens.

Pigeons courting, the cock
  Like an eighteenth-century marquis
Puffing his breast and dragging
  His fantail waltzwise;
O my love, the
  Southward trains are puffing.

Nursemaids gossiped,
  Sun was bright on pram-paint,
Gold in the breeze the arrow
  Swivelled on church-tops;
But Living drains the living
  Sieve we catch our gold in.

Toy sail skidding on Whitestone
  Pond at the peak of London,

Challenge of bells at morning,
  Crocus and almond;
O my love, my
  Thoughts avoid the challenge.

But the rumbling summer rolls
  A register behind us—
March to April to May
  To denser summer—
And the road is dusty, the goal
  Unknown we march to.

Rampant on Europe headlines
  Herald beasts of fable;
Backward the eyes to ancient
  Codes—vellum and roseleaf;
From the moving train of time the
  Fields move backward.

And now the searchlights
  Play their firemen's hoses,
Evil their purport
  Though their practice lovely,
Defence and death being always
  Collateral, coaeval.

And now the soldier
  Tightens belt and outlook,
Eyes on the target,
  Mind in the trigger-finger,
And a flight of lead connecting
  Self and horizon.

And now, and last, in London
   Poised on the edge of absence
I ask for a moment's mention
   Of days the days will cancel,
Though the long run may also
   Bring what we ask for.

[1938]

THE BRANDY GLASS

Only let it form within his hands once more—
The moment cradled like a brandy glass.
Sitting alone in the empty dining hall . . .
From the chandeliers the snow begins to fall
Piling around carafes and table legs
And chokes the passage of the revolving door.
The last diner, like a ventriloquist's doll
Left by his master, gazes before him, begs:
'Only let it form within my hands once more.'

[1937]

DAEMONIUM

Thank you, my friendly daemon, close to me as my
   shadow
For the mealy buttercup days in the ancient meadow,
For the days of my teens, the sluice of hearing and see-
   ing,
The days of topspin drives and physical well-being.

151

Thank you, my friend, shorter by a head, more placid
Than me your protégé whose ways are not so lucid,
My animal angel sure of touch and humour
With face still tanned from some primaeval summer.

Thanks for your sensual poise, your gay assurance,
Who skating on the lovely wafers of appearance
Have held my hand, put vetoes upon my reason,
Sent me to look for berries in the proper season.

Some day you will leave me or, at best, less often
I shall sense your presence when eyes and nostrils open,
Less often find your burgling fingers ready
To pick the locks when mine are too unsteady.

Thank you for the times of contact, for the glamour
Of pleasure sold by the clock and under the hammer,
Thank you for bidding for me, for breaking the cordon
Of spies and sentries round the unravished garden.

And thank you for the abandon of your giving,
For seeing in the dark, for making this life worth living.

[1937]

TAKEN FOR GRANTED

Taken for granted
   The household orbit in childhood
The punctual sound of the gong
   The round of domestic service.

152

The lamps were trimmed at six,
   Sticks were lavish for firewood,
The cat made bread of my knees,
   The housewife shopped in the morning.

The shops were fragrant, the blistered
   Vagrant peered in the windows
At tripes like deep-sea plants,
   Sausages in ropes of marble.

On the knees of bountiful gods
   We lived in the ease of acceptance
Taking until we were twenty
   God's plenty for granted.

[1937]

HIDDEN ICE

There are few songs for domesticity
For routine work, money-making or scholarship
Though these are apt for eulogy or for tragedy.

And I would praise our adaptability
Who can spend years and years in offices and beds
Every morning twirling the napkin ring,
A twitter of inconsequent vitality.

And I would praise our inconceivable stamina
Who work to the clock and calendar and maintain
The equilibrium of nerves and notions,
Our mild bravado in the face of time.

153

Those who ignore disarm. The domestic ambush
The pleated lampshade the defeatist clock
May never be consummated and we may never
Strike on the rock beneath the calm upholstering.

But some though buoyed by habit, though convoyed
By habitual faces and hands that help the food
Or help one with one's coat, have lost their bearings
Struck hidden ice or currents no one noted.

One was found like Judas kissing flowers
And one who sat between the clock and the sun
Lies like a Saint Sebastian full of arrows
Feathered from his own hobby, his pet hours.

[1936]

CHESS

At the penultimate move, their saga nearly sung,
They have worked so hard to prove what lads they were
    when young,
Have looked up every word in order to be able to say
The gay address unheard when they were dumb and gay.
Your Castle to King's Fourth under your practised hand!
What is the practice worth, so few being left to stand?
Better the raw levies jostling in the square
Than two old men in a crevice sniping at empty air;
The veterans on the pavement puff their cheeks and blow
The music of enslavement that echoes back 'I told you
    so';

The chapped hands fumble flutes, the tattered posters
    cry
Their craving for recruits who have not had time to die.
While our armies differ they move and feel the sun,
The victor is a cypher once the war is won.
Choose your gambit, vary the tactics of your game,
You move in a closed ambit that always ends the same.

[1937]

CIRCUS

I

Trapezists

Intricacy of engines,
Delicacy of darkness;
They rise into the tent's
Top like deep-sea divers

And hooked from the mouth like fish
Frame their frolic
Above the silent music
And the awed audience,

Hang by their teeth
Beneath the cone of canvas,
The ring beneath them
An eye that is empty

Who live in a world
Of aery technic
Like dolls or angels
Sexless and simple

Our fear their frame,
Hallowed by handclaps,
Honoured by eyes
Upward in incense.

On the tent's walls
Fourfold shadowed
In a crucifixion's
Endless moment

Intricacy of,
Delicacy of,
Darkness and engines.

II

Horses

The long whip lingers,
Toys with the sawdust;
The horses amble
On a disc of dreams.

The drumsticks flower
In pink percussion
To mix with the metal
Petals of brass.

156

The needle runs
In narrower circles;
The long whip leaps
And leads them inward.

Piebald horses
And ribald music
Circle around
A spangled lady.

III

Clowns

Clowns, Clowns and
Clowns
A firm that furthers
Nobody's business

Zanies by royal
Charter and adept
At false addition
And gay combustion

With bladders for batons
And upright eyebrows
Flappers for feet
And figs for no one.

The child's face pops
Like ginger beer
To see the air
Alive with bowlers.

Bric-a-brac
Pick-a-back
Spillbucket
Splits.

IV

Elephants

Tonnage of instinctive
Wisdom in tinsel,
Trunks like questions
And legs like tree trunks

On each forehead
A buxom blonde
And round each leg
A jangle of bells,

Deep in each brain
A chart of tropic
Swamp and twilight
Of creepered curtains,

Shamble in shoddy
Finery forward
And make their salaams
To the tiers of people—

Dummies with a reflex
Muscle of laughter
When they see the mountains
Come to Mahomet . . .
158

Efficacy of engines,
Obstinacy of darkness.

[1937]

RUGBY FOOTBALL EXCURSION

Euston—the smell of soot and fish and petrol;
Then in the train jogging and jogging,
The sheaf of wires from pole to pole beside us
Dogging the fancy northward

And waking to board the *Hibernia*—Bass and Guinness,
Bull-necks and brogues and favours
And Kerry-coloured girls; the whole excursion
Savours of twelve years back

Back to my adolescence, back to Ireland,
'Ilkla Moor ba't a't' from Midland voices,
And Wicklow apricot in early sunshine
Rejoices what was jaded.

Horse-cabs and outside cars—the ballyhoo for trippers—
And College Park reposeful behind the railings;
Emphatic old ladies' voices in a lounge lamenting
Failings of health and budgets.

Lansdowne Road—the swirl of faces, flags,
Gilbert and Sullivan music, emerald jerseys;
Spire and crane beyond remind the mind on furlough
Of Mersey's code and Rome's.

159

Eccentric scoring—Nicholson, Marshall and Unwin,
Replies by Bailey and Daly;
Rugs around our shins, the effortless place-kick
Gaily carving the goalposts.

Then tea and toast with Fellows and Bishops in a huge
Regency room in the warmth of a classic assurance
Looking on Stephen's Green where they blew up George
    the Second—
Endurance of one-way thinking.

And then a walk through Dublin down the great
Grey streets broad and straight and drowned in twilight,
Statues of poets and Anglo-Irish patriots—
High lights of merged traditions.

Junkshops, the smell of poverty, pubs at the corner,
A chimney on fire and street on street of broken
Fanlights over the doors of tenement houses——
Token of the days of Reason.

In a frame from Sir Isaac Newton the dusk of Ireland
Bathes the children whipping their tops on the cobbles
Or swinging by ropes from a lamp post while a cripple
Hobbles like a Hogarth sketch.

These I must leave, rejoin the beery trippers
Whose other days prefer to-day delirious
Packing the bar on the boat, while a sapphire pinhead
Sirius marks Dun Laoghaire.

[1938]

160

CHRISTMAS SHOPPING

Spending beyond their income on gifts for Christmas—
Swing doors and crowded lifts and draperied jungles—
What shall we buy for our husbands and sons
    Different from last year?

Foxes hang by their noses behind plate glass—
Scream of macaws across festoons of paper—
Only the faces on the boxes of chocolates are free
    From boredom and crowsfeet.

Sometimes a chocolate box girl escapes in the flesh,
Lightly manoeuvres the crowd, trilling with laughter;
After a couple of years her feet and her brain will
    Tire like the others.

The great windows marshal their troops for assault on
      the purse,
Something-and-eleven the yard, hoodwinking logic,
The eleventh hour draining the gurgling pennies
    Down to the conduits

Down to the sewers of money—rats and marshgas—
Bubbling in maundering music under the pavement;
Here go the hours of routine, the weight on our eyelids—
    Pennies on corpses'.

While over the street in the centrally heated public
Library dwindling figures with sloping shoulders
And hands in pockets, weighted in the boots like chess-
      men,
    Stare at the printed

Columns of ads, the quickset road to riches,
Starting at a little and temporary but once we're
Started who knows whether we shan't continue,
  Salaries rising,

Rising like a salmon against the bullnecked river,
Bound for the spawning-ground of care-free days—
Good for a fling before the golden wheels run
  Down to a standstill.

And Christ is born—The nursery glad with baubles,
Alive with light and washable paint and children's
Eyes expects as its due the accidental
  Loot of a system.

Smell of the South—oranges in silver paper,
Dates and ginger, the benison of firelight,
The blue flames dancing round the brandied raisins,
  Smiles from above them,

Hands from above them as of gods but really
These their parents, always seen from below, them-
Selves are always anxious looking across the
  Fence to the future—

Out there lies the future gathering quickly
Its blank momentum; through the tubes of London
The dead winds blow the crowds like beasts in flight from
  Fire in the forest.

The little firtrees palpitate with candles
In hundreds of chattering households where the suburb
Straggles like nervous handwriting, the margin
  Blotted with smokestacks.

162

Further out on the coast the lighthouse moves its
Arms of light through the fog that wads our welfare,
Moves its arms like a giant at Swedish drill whose
  Mind is a vacuum.

[1937]

BAGPIPE MUSIC

It's no go the merry-go-round, it's no go the rickshaw,
All we want is a limousine and a ticket for the peepshow.
Their knickers are made of crêpe-de-chine, their shoes
    are made of python,
Their halls are lined with tiger rugs and their walls with
    heads of bison.

John MacDonald found a corpse, put it under the sofa,
Waited till it came to life and hit it with a poker,
Sold its eyes for souvenirs, sold its blood for whiskey,
Kept its bones for dumb-bells to use when he was fifty.

It's no go the Yogi-Man, it's no go Blavatsky,
All we want is a bank balance and a bit of skirt in a taxi.

Annie MacDougall went to milk, caught her foot in the
    heather,
Woke to hear a dance record playing of Old Vienna.
It's no go your maidenheads, it's no go your culture,
All we want is a Dunlop tyre and the devil mend the
    puncture.

163

The Laird o' Phelps spent Hogmannay declaring he was
     sober;
Counted his feet to prove the fact and found he had one
     foot over.
Mrs. Carmichael had her fifth, looked at the job with
     repulsion,
Said to the midwife 'Take it away; I'm through with
     overproduction.'

It's no go the gossip column, it's no go the Ceilidh,
All we want is a mother's help and a sugar-stick for the
     baby.

Willie Murray cut his thumb, couldn't count the damage,
Took the hide of an Ayrshire cow and used it for a
     bandage.
His brother caught three hundred cran when the seas
     were lavish,
Threw the bleeders back in the sea and went upon the
     parish.

It's no go the Herring Board, it's no go the Bible,
All we want is a packet of fags when our hands are idle.

It's no go the picture palace, it's no go the stadium,
It's no go the country cot with a pot of pink geraniums.
It's no go the Government grants, it's no go the elections,
Sit on your arse for fifty years and hang your hat on a
     pension.

It's no go my honey love, it's no go my poppet;
Work your hands from day to day, the winds will blow
     the profit.

The glass is falling hour by hour, the glass will fall for
 ever,
But if you break the bloody glass you won't hold up the
 weather.

[1937]

VI
AUTUMN JOURNAL: 1938

i

Close and slow, summer is ending in Hampshire,
    Ebbing away down ramps of shaven lawn where close-
        clipped yew
Insulates the lives of retired generals and admirals
    And the spyglasses hung in the hall and the prayer-
        books ready in the pew
And August going out to the tin trumpets of nasturtiums
    And the sunflowers' Salvation Army blare of brass
And the spinster sitting in a deck-chair picking up stitches
    Not raising her eyes to the noise of the planes that pass
Northward from Lee-on-Solent. Macrocarpa and cypress
    And roses on a rustic trellis and mulberry trees
And bacon and eggs in a silver dish for breakfast
    And all the inherited assets of bodily ease
And all the inherited worries, rheumatism and taxes,
    And whether Stella will marry and what to do with
        Dick
    And the branch of the family that lost their money in
        Hatry
    And the passing of the *Morning Post* and of life's
        climacteric
And the growth of vulgarity, cars that pass the gate-lodge
    And crowds undressing on the beach
And the hiking cockney lovers with thoughts directed
    Neither to God nor Nation but each to each.
But the home is still a sanctum under the pelmets,
    All quiet on the Family Front,
Farmyard noises across the fields at evening

While the trucks of the Southern Railway dawdle
    . . . shunt
Into poppy sidings for the night—night which knows no
    passion
    No assault of hands or tongue
For all is old as flint or chalk or pine-needles
    And the rebels and the young
Have taken the train to town or the two-seater
    Unravelling rails or road,
Losing the thread deliberately behind them—
    Autumnal palinode.
And I am in the train too now and summer is going
    South as I go north
Bound for the dead leaves falling, the burning bonfire,
    The dying that brings forth
The harder life, revealing the trees' girders,
    The frost that kills the germs of *laissez faire;*
West Meon, Tisted, Farnham, Woking, Weybridge,
    Then London's packed and stale and pregnant air.
My dog, a symbol of the abandoned order,
    Lies on the carriage floor,
Her eyes inept and glamorous as a film star's,
    Who wants to live, i.e. wants more
Presents, jewellery, furs, gadgets, solicitations
    As if to live were not
Following the curve of a planet or controlled water
    But a leap in the dark, a tangent, a stray shot.
It is this we learn after so many failures,
    The building of castles in sand, of queens in snow,
That we cannot make any corner in life or in life's beauty,
    That no river is a river which does not flow.

Surbiton, and a woman gets in, painted
  With dyed hair but a ladder in her stocking and eyes
Patient beneath the calculated lashes,
  Inured for ever to surprise;
And the train's rhythm becomes the *ad nauseam* repetition
  Of every tired aubade and maudlin madrigal,
The faded airs of sexual attraction
  Wandering like dead leaves along a warehouse wall:
'I loved my love with a platform ticket,
  A jazz song,
A handbag, a pair of stockings of Paris Sand—
  I loved her long.
I loved her between the lines and against the clock,
  Not until death
But till life did us part I loved her with paper money
  And with whiskey on the breath.
I loved her with peacock's eyes and the wares of
      Carthage,
  With glass and gloves and gold and a powder puff
With blasphemy, camaraderie, and bravado
  And lots of other stuff.
I loved my love with the wings of angels
  Dipped in henna, unearthly red,
With my office hours, with flowers and sirens,
  With my budget, my latchkey, and my daily bread.'
And so to London and down the ever-moving
      Stairs
Where a warm wind blows the bodies of men together
  And blows apart their complexes and cares.

Spider, spider, twisting tight—
    But the watch is wary beneath the pillow—
I am afraid in the web of night
    When the window is fingered by the shadows of
        branches,
When the lions roar beneath the hill
    And the meter clicks and the cistern bubbles
And the gods are absent and the men are still—
    Noli me tangere, my soul is forfeit.
Some now are happy in the hive of home,
    Thigh over thigh and a light in the night nursery,
And some are hungry under the starry dome
    And some sit turning handles.
Glory to God in the Lowest, peace beneath the earth,
    Dumb and deaf at the nadir;
I wonder now whether anything is worth
    The eyelid opening and the mind recalling.
And I think of Persephone gone down to dark,
    No more a virgin, gone the garish meadow,
But why must she come back, why must the snowdrop
        mark
    That life goes on for ever?
There are nights when I am lonely and long for love
    But to-night is quintessential dark forbidding
Anyone beside or below me; only above
    Pile high the tumulus, good-bye to starlight.
Good-bye the Platonic sieve of the Carnal Man
    But good-bye also Plato's philosophising;
I have a better plan

To hit the target straight without circumlocution.
If you can equate Being in its purest form
    With denial of all appearance,
Then let me disappear—the scent grows warm
    For pure Not-Being, Nirvana.
Only the spider spinning out his reams
    Of colourless thread says Only there are always
Interlopers, dreams,
    Who let no dead dog lie nor death be final;
Suggesting, while he spins, that to-morrow will out-
        weigh
    To-night, that Becoming is a match for Being,
That to-morrow is also a day,
    That I must leave my bed and face the music.
As all the others do who with a grin
    Shake off sleep like a dog and hurry to desk or engine
And the fear of life goes out as they clock in
    And history is reasserted.
Spider, spider, your irony is true;
    Who am I—or I—to demand oblivion?
I must go out to-morrow as the others do
    And build the falling castle;
Which has never fallen, thanks
    Not to any formula, red tape or institution,
Not to any creeds or banks,
    But to the human animal's endless courage.
Spider, spider, spin
    Your register and let me sleep a little,
Not now in order to end but to begin
    The task begun so often.

August is nearly over, the people
  Back from holiday are tanned
With blistered thumbs and a wallet of snaps and a little
  Joie de vivre which is contraband;
Whose stamina is enough to face the annual
  Wait for the annual spree,
Whose memories are stamped with specks of sunshine
  Like faded *fleurs de lys*.
Now the till and the typewriter call the fingers,
  The workman gathers his tools
For the eight-hour day but after that the solace
  Of films or football pools
Or of the gossip or cuddle, the moments of self-glory
  Or self-indulgence, blinkers on the eyes of doubt,
The blue smoke rising and the brown lace sinking
  In the empty glass of stout.
Most are accepters, born and bred to harness,
  And take things as they come,
But some refusing harness and more who are refused it
  Would pray that another and a better Kingdom come,
Which now is sketched in the air or travestied in slogans
  Written in chalk or tar on stucco or plaster-board
But in time may find its body in men's bodies,
  Its law and order in their hearts' accord,
Where skill will no longer languish nor energy be
      trammelled
  To competition and graft,
Exploited in subservience but not allegiance
  To an utterly lost and daft
System that gives a few at fancy prices

Their fancy lives
While ninety-nine in the hundred who never attend the
    banquet
  Must wash the grease of ages off the knives.
And now the tempter whispers 'But you also
  Have the slave-owner's mind,
Would like to sleep on a mattress of easy profits,
  To snap your fingers or a whip and find
Servants or houris ready to wince and flatter
  And build with their degradation your self-esteem;
What you want is not a world of the free in function
  But a niche at the top, the skimmings of the cream.'
And I answer that that is largely so for habit makes me
  Think victory for one implies another's defeat,
That freedom means the power to order, and that in order
  To preserve the values dear to the élite
The élite must remain a few. It is so hard to imagine
  A world where the many would have their chance
    without
A fall in the standard of intellectual living
  And nothing left that the highbrow cared about.
Which fears must be suppressed. There is no reason for
    thinking
  That, if you give a chance to people to think or live,
The arts of thought or life will suffer and become rougher
  And not return more than you could ever give.
And now I relapse to sleep, to dreams perhaps and re-
    action
  Where I shall play the gangster or the sheikh,
Kill for the love of killing, make the world my sofa,
  Unzip the women and insult the meek.
Which fantasies no doubt are due to my private history,

Matter for the analyst,
But the final cure is not in his past-dissecting fingers
    But in a future of action, the will and fist
Of those who abjure the luxury of self-pity,
    And prefer to risk a movement without being sure
If movement would be better or worse in a hundred
    Years or a thousand when their heart is pure.
None of our hearts are pure, we always have mixed
        motives,
    Are self deceivers, but the worst of all
Deceits is to murmur 'Lord, I am not worthy'
    And, lying easy, turn your face to the wall.
But may I cure that habit, look up and outwards
    And may my feet follow my wider glance
First no doubt to stumble, then to walk with the others
    And in the end—with time and luck—to dance.

iv

September has come and I wake
    And I think with joy how whatever, now or in future,
        the system
Nothing whatever can take
    The people away, there will always be people
For friends or for lovers though perhaps
    The conditions of love will be changed and its vices
        diminished
And affection not lapse
    To narrow possessiveness, jealousy founded on vanity.
September has come, it is *hers*
    Whose vitality leaps in the autumn,

176

Whose nature prefers
　　Trees without leaves and a fire in the fire-place;
So I give her this month and the next
　　Though the whole of my year should be hers who has
　　　　rendered already
So many of its days intolerable or perplexed
　　But so many more so happy;
Who has left a scent on my life and left my walls
　　Dancing over and over with her shadow,
Whose hair is twined in all my waterfalls
　　And all of London littered with remembered kisses.
So I am glad
　　That life contains her with her moods and moments
More shifting and more transient than I had
　　Yet thought of as being integral to beauty;
Whose mind is like the wind on a sea of wheat,
　　Whose eyes are candour,
And assurance in her feet
　　Like a homing pigeon never by doubt diverted.
To whom I send my thanks
　　That the air has become shot silk, the streets are music,
And that the ranks
　　Of men are ranks of men, no more of cyphers.
So that if now alone
　　I must pursue this life, it will not be only
A drag from numbered stone to numbered stone
　　But a ladder of angels, river turning tidal.
Offhand, at times hysterical, abrupt,
　　You are one I always shall remember,
Whom cant can never corrupt
　　Nor argument disinherit.

Frivolous, always in a hurry, forgetting the address,
    Frowning too often, taking enormous notice
Of hats and backchat—how could I assess
    The thing that makes you different?
You whom I remember glad or tired,
    Smiling in drink or scintillating anger,
Inopportunely desired
    On boats, on trains, on roads when walking.
Sometimes untidy, often elegant,
    So easily hurt, so readily responsive,
To whom a trifle could be an irritant
    Or could be balm and manna.
Whose words would tumble over each other and pelt
    From pure excitement,
Whose fingers curl and melt
    When you were friendly.
I shall remember you in bed with bright
    Eyes or in a café stirring coffee
Abstractedly and on your plate the white
    Smoking stub your lips had touched with crimson.
And I shall remember how your words could hurt
    Because they were so honest
And even your lies were able to assert
    Integrity of purpose.
And it is on the strength of knowing you
    I reckon generous feeling more important
Than the mere deliberating what to do
    When neither the pros nor cons affect the pulses.
And though I have suffered from your special strength
    Who never flatter for points nor fake responses,
I should be proud if I could evolve at length
    An equal thrust and pattern.

To-day was a beautiful day, the sky was a brilliant
    Blue for the first time for weeks and weeks
But posters flapping on the railings tell the fluttered
    World that Hitler speaks, that Hitler speaks
And we cannot take it in and we go to our daily
    Jobs to the dull refrain of the caption 'War'
Buzzing around us as from hidden insects
    And we think 'This must be wrong, it has happened
        before,
Just like this before, we must be dreaming;
    It was long ago these flies
Buzzed like this, so why are they still bombarding
    The ears if not the eyes?'
And we laugh it off and go round town in the evening
    And this, we say, is on me;
Something out of the usual, a Pimm's Number One, a
        Picon—
    But did you see
The latest? You mean whether Cobb has bust the record
    Or do you mean the Australians have lost their last by
        ten
Wickets or do you mean that the autumn fashions—
    No, we don't mean anything like that again.
No, what we mean is Hodza, Henlein, Hitler,
    The Maginot Line,
The heavy panic that cramps the lungs and presses
    The collar down the spine.
And when we go out into Piccadilly Circus
    They are selling and buying the late
Special editions snatched and read abruptly

Beneath the electric signs as crude as Fate.
And the individual, powerless, has to exert the
    Powers of will and choice
And choose between enormous evils, either
    Of which depends on somebody else's voice.
The cylinders are racing in the presses,
    The mines are laid,
The ribbon plumbs the fallen fathoms of Wall Street,
    And you and I are afraid.
To-day they were building in Oxford Street, the mortar
    Pleasant to smell,
But now it seems futility, imbecility,
    To be building shops when nobody can tell
What will happen next. What will happen
    We ask and waste the question on the air;
Nelson is stone and Johnnie Walker moves his
    Legs like a cretin over Trafalgar Square.
And in the Corner House the carpet-sweepers
    Advance between the tables after crumbs
Inexorably, like a tank battalion
    In answer to the drums.
In Tottenham Court Road the tarts and Negroes
    Loiter beneath the lights
And the breeze gets colder as on so many other
    September nights.
A smell of French bread in Charlotte Street, a rustle
    Of leaves in Regent's Park
And suddenly from the Zoo I hear a sea-lion
    Confidently bark.
And so to my flat with the trees outside the window
    And the dahlia shapes of the lights on Primrose Hill
Whose summit once was used for a gun emplacement

And very likely will
Be used that way again. The bloody frontier
   Converges on our beds
Like jungle beaters closing in on their destined
   Trophy of pelts and heads.
And at this hour of the day it is no good saying
   'Take away this cup';
Having helped to fill it ourselves it is only logic
   That now we should drink it up.
Nor can we hide our heads in the sands, the sands have
   Filtered away;
Nothing remains but rock at this hour, this zero
   Hour of the day.
Or that is how it seems to me as I listen
   To a hooter call at six
And then a woodpigeon calls and stops but the wind
      continues
   Playing its dirge in the trees, playing its tricks.
And now the dairy cart comes clopping slowly—
   Milk at the doors—
And factory workers are on their way to factories
   And charwomen to chores.
And I notice feathers sprouting from the rotted
   Silk of my black
Double eiderdown which was a wedding
   Present eight years back.
And the linen which I lie on came from Ireland
   In the easy days
When all I thought of was affection and comfort,
   Petting and praise.
And now the woodpigeon starts again denying
   The values of the town

And a car having crossed the hill accelerates, changes
    Up, having just changed down.
And a train begins to chug and I wonder what the morn-
    ing
    Paper will say,
And decide to go quickly to sleep for the morning al-
    ready
Is with us, the day is to-day.

vi

And I remember Spain
    At Easter ripe as an egg for revolt and ruin
Though for a tripper the rain
    Was worse than the surly or the worried or the haunted
        faces
With writings on the walls—
    Hammer and sickle, Boicot, Viva, Muerra;
With café-au-lait brimming the waterfalls,
    With sherry, shellfish, omelettes;
With fretted stone the Moor
    Had chiselled for effects of sun and shadow;
With shadows of the poor,
    The begging cripples and the children begging.
The churches full of saints
    Tortured on racks of marble—
The old complaints
    Covered with gilt and dimly lit with candles.
With powerful or banal
    Monuments of riches or repression
And the Escorial
    Cold for ever within like the heart of Philip.

With ranks of dominoes
  Deployed on café tables the whole of Sunday;
With cabarets that call the tourist, shows
  Of thighs and eyes and nipples.
With slovenly soldiers, nuns,
  And peeling posters from the last election
Promising bread or guns
  Or an amnesty or another
Order or else the old
  Glory veneered and varnished
As if veneer could hold
  The rotten guts and crumbled bones together.
And a vulture hung in air
  Below the cliffs of Ronda and below him
His hook-winged shadow wavered like despair
  Across the chequered vineyards.
And the boot-blacks in Madrid
  Kept us half an hour with polish and pincers
And all we did
  In that city was drink and think and loiter.
And in the Prado half-
  wit princes looked from the canvas they had paid for
(Goya had the laugh—
  But can what is corrupt be cured by laughter?)
And the day at Aranjuez
  When the sun came out for once on the yellow river
With Valdepeñas burdening the breath
  We slept a royal sleep in the royal gardens;
And at Toledo walked
  Around the ramparts where they throw the garbage
And glibly talked
  Of how the Spaniards lack all sense of business.

And Avila was cold
    And Segovia was picturesque and smelly
And a goat on the road seemed old
    As the rocks or the Roman arches.
And Easter was wet and full
    In Seville and in the ring on Easter Sunday
A clumsy bull and then a clumsy bull
    Nodding his banderillas died of boredom.
And the standard of living was low
    But that, we thought to ourselves, was not our busi-
        ness;
All that the tripper wants is the *status quo*
    Cut and dried for trippers.
And we thought the papers a lark
    With their party politics and blank invective;
And we thought the dark
    Women who dyed their hair should have it dyed more
        often.
And we sat in trains all night
    With the windows shut among civil guards and peas-
        ants
And tried to play piquet by a tiny light
    And tried to sleep bolt upright;
And cursed the Spanish rain
    And cursed their cigarettes which came to pieces
And caught heavy colds in Cordova and in vain
    Waited for the right light for taking photos.
And we met a Cambridge don who said with an air
    'There's going to be trouble shortly in this country,'
And ordered anise, pudgy and debonair,
    Glad to show off his mastery of the language.
But only an inch behind

184

This map of olive and ilex, this painted hoarding,
Careless of visitors the people's mind
    Was tunnelling like a mole to day and danger.
And the day before we left
    We saw the mob in flower at Algeciras
Outside a toothless door, a church bereft
    Of its images and its aura.
And at La Linea while
    The night put miles between us and Gibraltar
We heard the blood-lust of a drunkard pile
    His heaven high with curses;
And next day took the boat
    For home, forgetting Spain, not realising
That Spain would soon denote
    Our grief, our aspirations;
Not knowing that our blunt
    Ideals would find their whetstone, that our spirit
Would find its frontier on the Spanish front,
    Its body in a rag-tag army.

vii

Conferences, adjournments, ultimatums,
    Flights in the air, castles in the air,
The autopsy of treaties, dynamite under the bridges,
    The end of *laissez faire*.
After the warm days the rain comes pimpling
    The paving stones with white
And with the rain the national conscience, creeping,
    Seeping through the night.
And in the sodden park on Sunday protest
    Meetings assemble not, as so often, now

185

Merely to advertise some patent panacea
    But simply to avow
The need to hold the ditch; a bare avowal
    That may perhaps imply
Death at the doors in a week but perhaps in the long run
    Exposure of the lie.
Think of a number, double it, treble it, square it,
    And sponge it out
And repeat *ad lib.* and mark the slate with crosses;
    There is no time to doubt
If the puzzle really has an answer. Hitler yells on the
        wireless,
    The night is damp and still
And I hear dull blows on wood outside my window;
    They are cutting down the trees on Primrose Hill.
The wood is white like the roast flesh of chicken,
    Each tree falling like a closing fan;
No more looking at the view from seats beneath the
        branches,
    Everything is going to plan;
They want the crest of this hill for anti-aircraft,
    The guns will take the view
And searchlights probe the heavens for bacilli
    With narrow wands of blue.
And the rain came on as I watched the territorials
    Sawing and chopping and pulling on ropes like a team
In a village tug-of-war; and I found my dog had vanished
    And thought 'This is the end of the old régime,'
But found the police had got her at St. John's Wood sta-
        tion
    And fetched her in the rain and went for a cup
Of coffee to an all-night shelter and heard a taxi-driver

Say 'It turns me up
When I see them soldiers in lorries'—rumble of tumbrils
   Drums in the trees
Breaking the eardrums of the ravished dryads—
   It turns me up; a coffee, please.
And as I go out I see a windshield-wiper
   In an empty car
Wiping away like mad and I feel astounded
   That things have gone so far.
And I come back here to my flat and wonder whether
   From now on I need take
The trouble to go out choosing stuff for curtains
   As I don't know anyone to make
Curtains quickly. Rather one should quickly
   Stop the cracks for gas or dig a trench
And take one's paltry measures against the coming
   Of the unknown *Uebermensch*.
But one—meaning I—is bored, am bored, the issue
   Involving principle but bound in fact
To squander principle in panic and self-deception—
   Accessories after the act,
So that all we foresee is rivers in spate sprouting
   With drowning hands
And men like dead frogs floating till the rivers
   Lose themselves in the sands.
And we who have been brought up to think of 'Gallant
      Belgium'
   As so much blague
Are now preparing again to essay good through evil
   For the sake of Prague;
And must, we suppose, become uncritical, vindictive,
   And must, in order to beat

The enemy, model ourselves upon the enemy,
  A howling radio for our paraclete.
The night continues wet, the axe keeps falling,
  The hill grows bald and bleak
No longer one of the sights of London but maybe
  We shall have fireworks here by this day week.

viii

Sun shines easy, sun shines gay
  On bug-house, warehouse, brewery, market,
On the chocolate factory and the B.S.A.,
  On the Greek town hall and Josiah Mason;
On the Mitchells' and Butlers' Tudor pubs,
  On the white police and the one-way traffic
And glances off the chromium hubs
  And the metal studs in the sleek macadam.
Eight years back about this time
  I came to live in this hazy city
To work in a building caked with grime
  Teaching the classics to Midland students;
Virgil, Livy, the usual round,
  Principal parts and the lost digamma;
And to hear the prison-like lecture room resound
  To Homer in a Dudley accent.
But Life was comfortable, life was fine
  With two in a bed and patchwork cushions
And checks and tassels on the washing-line,
  A gramophone, a cat, and the smell of jasmine.
The steaks were tender, the films were fun,
  The walls were striped like a Russian ballet,
There were lots of things undone

But nobody cared, for the days were early.
Nobody niggled, nobody cared,
   The soul was deaf to the mounting debit,
The soul was unprepared
   But the firelight danced on the ply-wood ceiling.
We drove round Shropshire in a bijou car—
   Bewdley, Cleobury Mortimer, Ludlow—
And the map of England was a toy bazaar
   And the telephone wires were idle music.
And sun shone easy, sun shone hard
   On quickly dropping pear-tree blossom
And pigeons courting in the cobbled yard
   With flashing necks and notes of thunder.
We slept in linen, we cooked with wine,
   We paid in cash and took no notice
Of how the train ran down the line
   Into the sun against the signal.
We lived in Birmingham through the slump—
   Line your boots with a piece of paper—
Sunlight dancing on the rubbish dump,
   On the queues of men and the hungry chimneys.
And the next election came—
   Labour defeats in Erdington and Aston;
And life went on—for us went on the same;
   Who were we to count the losses?
Some went back to work and the void
   Took on shape while others climbing
The uphill nights of the unemployed
   Woke in the morning to factory hooters.
Little on the plate and nothing in the post;
   Queue in the rain or try the public
Library where the eye may coast

Columns of print for a hopeful harbour.
But roads ran easy, roads ran gay
    Clear of the city and we together
Could put on tweeds for a getaway
    South or west to Clee or the Cotswolds;
Forty to the gallon; into the green
    Fields in the past of English history;
Flies in the bonnet and dust on the screen
    And no look back to the burning city.
That was then and now is now,
    Here again on a passing visit,
Passing through but how
    Memory blocks the passage.
Just as in 1931
    Sun shines easy but I no longer
Docket a place in the sun—
    No wife, no ivory tower, no funk-hole.
The night grows purple, the crisis hangs
    Over the roofs like a Persian army
And all of Xenophon's parasangs
    Would take us only an inch from danger.
Black-out practice and A.R.P.,
    Newsboys driving a roaring business,
The flapping paper snatched to see
    If anything has, or has not, happened.
And I go to the Birmingham Hippodrome
    Packed to the roof and primed for laughter
And beautifully at home
    With the ukulele and the comic chestnuts;
'As pals we meet, as pals we part'—
    Embonpoint and a new tiara;
The comedian spilling the apple-cart

Of *doubles entendres* and doggerel verses.
And the next day begins
  Again with alarm and anxious
Listening to bulletins
  From distant, measured voices
Arguing for peace
  While the zero hour approaches,
While the eagles gather and the petrol and oil and grease
  Have all been applied and the vultures back the eagles.
But once again
  The crisis is put off and things look better
And we feel negotiation is not vain—
  Save my skin and damn my conscience.
And negotiation wins,
  If you can call it winning,
And here we are—just as before—safe in our skins;
  Glory to God for Munich.
And stocks go up and wrecks
  Are salved and politicians' reputations
Go up like Jack-on-the-Beanstalk; only the Czechs
  Go down and without fighting.

ix

Now we are back to normal, now the mind is
  Back to the even tenor of the usual day
Skidding no longer across the uneasy camber
  Of the nightmare way.
We are safe though others have crashed the railings
  Over the river ravine; their wheel-tracks carve the
     bank
But after the event all we can do is argue

191

And count the widening ripples where they sank.
October comes with rain whipping around the ankles
   In waves of white at night
And filling the raw clay trenches (the parks of London
   Are a nasty sight).
In a week I return to work, lecturing, coaching,
   As impresario of the Ancient Greeks
Who wore the chiton and lived on fish and olives
   And talked philosophy or smut in cliques;
Who believed in youth and did not gloze the unpleasant
   Consequences of age;
What is life, one said, or what is pleasant
   Once you have turned the page
Of love? The days grow worse, the dice are loaded
   Against the living man who pays in tears for breath;
Never to be born was the best, call no man happy
   This side death.
Conscious—long before Engels—of necessity
   And therein free
They plotted out their life with truism and humour
   Between the jealous heaven and the callous sea.
And Pindar sang the garland of wild olive
   And Alcibiades lived from hand to mouth
Double-crossing Athens, Persia, Sparta,
   And many died in the city of plague, and many of
      drouth
In Sicilian quarries, and many by the spear and arrow
   And many more who told their lies too late
Caught in the eternal factions and reactions
   Of the city-state.
And free speech shivered on the pikes of Macedonia
   And later on the swords of Rome

And Athens became a mere university city
    And the goddess born of the foam
Became the kept hetaera, heroine of Menander,
    And the philosopher narrowed his focus, confined
His efforts to putting his own soul in order
    And keeping a quiet mind.
And for a thousand years they went on talking,
    Making such apt remarks,
A race no longer of heroes but of professors
    And crooked business men and secretaries and clerks;
Who turned out dapper little elegiac verses
    On the ironies of fate, the transience of all
Affections, carefully shunning an over-statement
    But working the dying fall.
The Glory that was Greece: put it in a syllabus, grade it
    Page by page
To train the mind or even to point a moral
    For the present age:
Models of logic and lucidity, dignity, sanity,
    The golden mean between opposing ills
Though there were exceptions of course but only excep-
        tions—
    The bloody Bacchanals on the Thracian hills.
So the humanist in his room with Jacobean panels
    Chewing his pipe and looking on a lazy quad
Chops the Ancient World to turn a sermon
    To the greater glory of God.
But I can do nothing so useful or so simple;
    These dead are dead
And when I should remember the paragons of Hellas
    I think instead
Of the crooks, the adventurers, the opportunists,

The careless athletes and the fancy boys,
The hair-splitters, the pedants, the hard-boiled sceptics
  And the Agora and the noise
Of the demagogues and the quacks; and the women
      pouring
  Libations over graves
And the trimmers at Delphi and the dummies at Sparta
      and lastly
  I think of the slaves.
And how one can imagine oneself among them
  I do not know;
It was all so unimaginably different
  And all so long ago.

                    x

And so return to work—the M.A. gown,
  Alphas and Betas, central heating, floor-polish,
Demosthenes on the Crown
  And Oedipus at Colonus.
And I think of the beginnings of other terms
  Coming across the sea to unknown England
And memory reaffirms
  That alarm and exhilaration of arrival:
White wooden boxes, clatter of boots, a smell
  Of changing-rooms—Lifebuoy soap and muddy flan-
      nels—
And over all a bell
  Dragooning us to dormitory or classroom,
Ringing with a tongue of frost across the bare
  Benches and desks escutcheoned with initials;
We sat on the hot pipes by the wall, aware

Of the cold in our bones and the noise and the bell im-
      pending.
A fishtail gas-flare in the dark latrine;
   Chalk and ink and rows of pegs and lockers;
The War was on—maize and margarine
   And lessons on the map of Flanders.
But we had our toys—our electric torches, our glass
   Dogs and cats, and plasticine and conkers,
And we had our games, we learned to dribble and pass
   In jerseys striped like tigers.
And we had our make-believe, we had our mock
   Freedom in walks by twos and threes on Sunday,
We dug out fossils from the yellow rock
   Or drank the Dorset distance.
And we had our little tiptoe minds, alert
   To jump for facts and fancies and statistics
And our little jokes of Billy Bunter dirt
   And a heap of home-made dogma.
The Abbey chimes varnished the yellow street,
   The water from the taps in the bath was yellow,
The trees were full of owls, the sweets were sweet
   And life an expanding ladder.
And reading romances we longed to be grown up,
   To shoot from the hip and marry lovely ladies
And smoke cigars and live on claret cup
   And lie in bed in the morning;
Taking it for granted that things would still
   Get better and bigger and better and bigger and
      better,
That the road across the hill
   Led to the Garden of Eden;
Everything to expect and nothing to deplore,

Cushy days beyond the dumb horizon
And nothing to doubt about, to linger for
  In the halfway house of childhood.
And certainly we did not linger, we went on
  Growing and growing, gluttons for the future,
And four foot six was gone
  And we found it was time to be leaving
To be changing school, sandstone changed for chalk
  And ammonites for the flinty husks of sponges,
Another lingo to talk
  And jerseys in other colours.
And still the acquiring of unrelated facts,
  A string of military dates for history,
And the Gospels and the Acts
  And logarithms and Greek and the Essays of Elia;
And still the exhilarating rhythm of free
  Movement swimming or serving at tennis,
The fives-courts' tattling repartee
  Or rain on the sweating body.
But life began to narrow to what was done—
  The dominant gerundive—
And Number Two must mimic Number One
  In bearing, swearing, attitude and accent.
And so we jettisoned all
  Our childish fantasies and anarchism;
The weak must go to the wall
  But strength implies the system;
You must lose your soul to be strong, you cannot stand
  Alone on your own legs or your own ideas;
The order of the day is complete conformity and
  An automatic complacence.
Such was the order of the day; only at times

The Fool among the yes-men flashed his motley
To prick their pseudo-reason with his rhymes
  And drop his grain of salt on court behaviour.
And sometimes a whisper in books
  Would challenge the code, or a censored memory
      sometimes,
Sometimes the explosion of rooks,
  Sometimes the mere batter of light on the senses.
And the critic jailed in the mind would peep through the
      grate
  And husky from long silence, murmur gently
That there is something rotten in the state
  Of Denmark but the state is not the whole of Denmark;
And a spade is still a spade
  And the difference is not final between a tailored
Suit and a ready-made
  And knowledge is not—necessarily—wisdom;
And a cultured accent alone will not provide
  A season ticket to the Vita Nuova;
And there are many better men outside
  Than ever answered roll-call.
But the critic did not win, has not won yet
  Though always reminding us of points forgotten;
We hasten to forget
  As much as he remembers.
And school was what they always said it was,
  An apprenticeship to life, an initiation,
And all the better because
  The initiates were blindfold;
The reflex action of a dog or sheep
  Being enough for normal avocations
And life rotating in an office sleep

As long as things are normal.
Which it was assumed that they would always be;
    On that assumption terms began and ended;
And now, in 1938 A.D.,
    Term is again beginning.

xi

But work is alien; what do I care for the Master
    Of those who know, of those who know too much?
I am too harassed by my familiar devils,
    By those I cannot see, by those I may not touch;
Knowing perfectly well in the mind, on paper,
    How wasteful and absurd
Are personal fixations but yet the pulse keeps thrumming
    And her voice is faintly heard
Through walls and walls of indifference and abstraction
    And across the London roofs
And every so often calls up hopes from nowhere,
    A distant clatter of hoofs,
And my common sense denies she is returning
    And says, if she does return, she will not stay;
And my pride, in the name of reason, tells me to cut my
        losses
    And call it a day.
Which, if I had the cowardice of my convictions,
    I certainly should do
But doubt still finds a loophole
    To gamble on another rendezvous.
And I try to feel her in fancy but the fancy
    Dissolves in curls of mist
And I try to summarise her but how can hungry

Love be a proper analyst?
For suddenly I hate her and would murder
　　Her memory if I could
And then of a sudden I see her sleeping gently
　　Inaccessible in a sleeping wood
But thorns and thorns around her
　　And the cries of night
And I have no knife or axe to hack my passage
　　Back to the lost delight.
And then I think of the others and jealousy riots
　　In impossible schemes
To kill them with all the machinery of fact and with all
　　　the
　　Tortures of dreams.
But yet, my dear, if only for my own distraction,
　　I have to try to assess
Your beauty of body, your paradoxes of spirit,
　　Even your taste in dress.
Whose emotions are an intricate dialectic,
　　Whose eagerness to live
A many-sided life might be deplored as fickle,
　　Unpractical, or merely inquisitive.
A superficial comment; for your instinct
　　Sanctions all you do,
Who know that truth is nothing in abstraction,
　　That action makes both wish and principle come true;
Whose changes have the logic of a prism,
　　Whose moods create,
Who never linger haggling on the threshold,
　　To weigh the pros and cons until it is too late.
At times intractable, virulent, hypercritical,
　　With a bitter tongue;

Over-shy at times, morose, defeatist,
    At times a token that the world is young;
Given to over-statement, careless of caution,
    Quick to sound the chimes
Of delicate intuition, at times malicious
    And generous at times.
Whose kaleidoscopic ways are all authentic,
    Whose truth is not of a statement but of a dance
So that even when you deceive your deceits are merely
    Technical and of no significance.
And so, when I think of you, I have to meet you
    In thought on your own ground;
To apply to you my algebraic canons
    Would merely be unsound;
And, having granted this, I cannot balance
    My hopes or fears of you in pros and cons;
It has been proved that Achilles cannot catch the
        Tortoise,
    It has been proved that men are automatons,
Everything wrong has been proved. I will not bother
    Any more with proof;
I see the future glinting with your presence
    Like moon on a slate roof,
And my spirits rise again. It is October,
    The year-god dying on the destined pyre
With all the colours of a scrambled sunset
    And all the funeral elegance of fire
In the grey world to lie cocooned but shaping
    His gradual return;
No one can stop the cycle;
    The grate is full of ash but fire will always burn.
Therefore, listening to the taxis

(In which you never come) so regularly pass,
I wait content, banking on the spring and watching
    The dead leaves canter over the dowdy grass.

xii

These days are misty, insulated, mute
    Like a faded tapestry and the soft pedal
Is down and the yellow leaves are falling down
    And we hardly have the heart to meddle
Any more with personal ethics or public calls;
    People have not recovered from the crisis,
Their faces are far away, the tone of the words
    Belies their thesis.
For they say that now it is time unequivocally to act,
    To let the pawns be taken,
That criticism, a virtue previously,
    Now can only weaken
And that when we go to Rome
    We must do as the Romans do, cry out together
For bread and circuses; put on your togas now
    For this is Roman weather.
Circuses of death and from the topmost tiers
    A cataract of goggling, roaring faces;
On the arena sand
    Those who are about to die try out their paces.
Now it is night, a cold mist creeps, the night
    Is still and damp and lonely;
Sitting by the fire it is hard to realise
    That the legions wait at the gates and that there is only
A little time for rest though not by rights for rest,
    Rather for whetting the will, for calculating

201

A compromise between necessity and wish,
    Apprenticed late to learn the trade of hating.
Remember the sergeant barking at bayonet practice
    When you were small;
To kill a dummy you must act a dummy
    Or you cut no ice at all.
Now it is morning again, the 25th of October,
    In a white fog the cars have yellow lights;
The chill creeps up the wrists, the sun is sallow,
    The silent hours grow down like stalactites.
And reading Plato talking about his Forms
    To damn the artist touting round his mirror,
I am glad that I have been left the third best bed
    And live in a world of error.
His world of capital initials, of transcendent
    Ideas is too bleak;
For me there remain to all intents and purposes
    Seven days in the week
And no one Tuesday is another and you destroy it
    If you subtract the difference and relate
It merely to the Form of Tuesday. This is Tuesday
    The 25th of October, 1938.
Aristotle was better who watched the insect breed,
    The natural world develop,
Stressing the function, scrapping the Form in Itself,
    Taking the horse from the shelf and letting it gallop.
Education gives us too many labels
    And clichés, cuts too many Gordian knots;
Trains us to keep the roads nor reconnoitre
    Any of the beauty-spots or danger-spots.
Not that I would rather be a peasant; the Happy Peasant
    Like the Noble Savage is a myth;

I do not envy the self-possession of an elm-tree
    Nor the aplomb of a granite monolith.
All that I would like to be is human, having a share
    In a civilised, articulate and well-adjusted
Community where the mind is given its due
    But the body is not distrusted.
As it is, the so-called humane studies
    May lead to cushy jobs
But leave the men who land them spiritually bankrupt
    Intellectual snobs.
Not but what I am glad to have my comforts,
    Better authentic mammon than a bogus god;
If it were not for Lit. Hum. I might be climbing
    A ladder with a hod.
And seven hundred a year
    Will pay the rent and the gas and the phone and the
        grocer;
(The Emperor takes his seat beneath the awning,
    Those who are about to die . . .) Come, pull the cur-
        tains closer.

xiii

Which things being so, as we said when we studied
    The classics, I ought to be glad
That I studied the classics at Marlborough and Merton,
    Not everyone here having had
The privilege of learning a language
    That is incontrovertibly dead,
And of carting a toy-box of hall-marked marmoreal
        phrases
    Around in his head.

We wrote compositions in Greek which they said was a
    lesson
  In logic and good for the brain;
We marched, counter-marched to the field-marshal's
    blue-pencil baton,
  We dressed by the right and we wrote out the sentence
    again.
We learned that a gentleman never misplaces his accents,
  That nobody knows how to speak, much less how to
    write
English who has not hob-nobbed with the great-grand-
    parents of English,
  That the boy on the Modern Side is merely a parasite
But the classical student is bred to the purple, his training
    in syntax
  Is also a training in thought
And even in morals; if called to the bar or the barracks
  He always will do what he ought.
And knowledge, besides, should be prized for the sake
    of knowledge:
  Oxford crowded the mantelpiece with gods—
Scaliger, Heinsius, Dindorf, Bentley and Wilamowitz—
  As we learned our genuflexions for Honour Mods.
And then they taught us philosophy, logic and meta-
    physics,
  The Negative Judgment and the *Ding an sich,*
And every single thinker was powerful as Napoleon
  And crafty as Metternich.
And it really was very attractive to be able to talk about
    tables
  And to ask if the table *is,*
And to draw the cork out of an old conundrum

And watch the paradoxes fizz.
And it made one confident to think that nothing
    Really was what it seemed under the sun,
That the actual was not real and the real was not with us
    And all that mattered was the One.
And they said 'The man in the street is so naïve, he never
    Can see the wood for the trees;
He thinks he knows he sees a thing but cannot
    Tell you how he knows the thing he thinks he sees.'
And oh how much I liked the Concrete Universal,
    I never thought that I should
Be telling them vice-versa
    That they can't see the trees for the wood.
But certainly it was fun while it lasted
    And I got my honours degree
And was stamped as a person of intelligence and culture
    For ever wherever two or three
Persons of intelligence and culture
    Are gathered together in talk
Writing definitions on invisible blackboards
    In non-existent chalk.
But such sacramental occasions
    Are nowadays comparatively rare;
There is always a wife or a boss or a dun or a client
    Disturbing the air.
Barbarians always, life in the particular always,
    Dozens of men in the street,
And the perennial if unimportant problem
    Of getting enough to eat.
So blow the bugles over the metaphysicians,
    Let the pure mind return to the Pure Mind;
I must be content to remain in the world of Appearance

And sit on the mere appearance of a behind.
But in case you should think my education was wasted
    I hasten to explain
That having once been to the University of Oxford
    You can never really again
Believe anything that anyone says and that of course is
        an asset
    In a world like ours;
Why bother to water a garden
    That is planted with paper flowers?
O the Freedom of the Press, the Late Night Final,
    To-morrow's pulp;
One should not gulp one's port but as it isn't
    Port, I'll gulp it if I want to gulp
But probably I'll just enjoy the colour
    And pour it down the sink
For I don't call advertisement a statement
    Or any quack medicine a drink.
Good-bye now, Plato and Hegel,
    The shop is closing down;
They don't want any philosopher-kings in England,
    There ain't no universals in this man's town.

xiv

The next day I drove by night
    Among red and amber and green, spears and candles,
Corkscrews and slivers of reflected light
    In the mirror of the rainy asphalt
Along the North Circular and the Great West roads
    Running the gauntlet of impoverished fancy
Where housewives bolster up their jerry-built abodes

With *amour propre* and the habit of Hire Purchase.
The wheels whished in the wet, the flashy strings
    Of neon lights unravelled, the windshield-wiper
Kept at its job like a tiger in a cage or a cricket that sings
    All night through for nothing.
Factory, a site for a factory, rubbish dumps,
    Bungalows in lath and plaster, in brick, in concrete,
And shining semi-circles of petrol pumps
    Like intransigent gangs of idols.
And the road swings round my head like a lassoo
    Looping wider and wider tracts of darkness
And the country succeeds the town and the country too
    Is damp and dark and evil.
And coming over the Chilterns the dead leaves leap
    Charging the windshield like a barrage of angry
Birds as I take the steep
    Plunge to Henley or Hades.
And at the curves of the road the telephone wires
    Shine like strands of silk and the hedge solicits
My irresponsible tyres
    To an accident, to a bed in the wet grasses.
And in quiet crooked streets only the village pub
    Spills a golden puddle
Over the pavement and trees bend down and rub
    Unopened dormer windows with their knuckles.
Nettlebed, Shillingford, Dorchester—each unrolls
    The road to Oxford; *Qu'allais-je faire* to-morrow
Driving voters to the polls
    In that home of lost illusions?
And what am I doing it for?
    Mainly for fun, partly for a half-believed-in
Principle, a core

Of fact in a pulp of verbiage,
Remembering that this crude and so-called obsolete
    Top-heavy tedious parliamentary system
Is our only ready weapon to defeat
    The legions' eagles and the lictors' axes;
And remembering that those who by their habit hate
    Politics can no longer keep their private
Values unless they open the public gate
    To a better political system.
That Rome was not built in a day is no excuse
    For *laissez faire,* for bowing to the odds against us;
What is the use
    Of asking what is the use of one brick only:
The perfectionist stands for ever in a fog
    Waiting for the fog to clear; better to be vulgar
And use your legs and leave a blank for Hogg
    And put a cross for Lindsay.
There are only too many who say 'What difference does
        it make
    One way or the other?
To turn the stream of history will take
    More than a by-election.'
So Thursday came and Oxford went to the polls
    And made its coward vote and the streets resounded
To the triumphant cheers of the lost souls—
    The profiteers, the dunderheads, the smarties.
And I drove back to London in the dark of the morning,
        the trees
    Standing out in the headlights cut from cardboard;
Wondering which disease
    Is worse—the Status Quo or the Mere Utopia.
For from now on

Each occasion must be used, however trivial,
To rally the ranks of those whose chance will soon be
    gone
  For even guerrilla warfare.
The nicest people in England have always been the least
  Apt to solidarity or alignment
But all of them must now align against the beast
  That prowls at every door and barks in every headline.
Dawn and London and daylight and last the sun:
  I stop the car and take the yellow placard
Off the bonnet; that little job is done
  Though without success or glory.
The plane-tree leaves come sidling down
  (Catch my guineas, catch my guineas)
And the sun caresses Camden Town,
  The barrows of oranges and apples.

xv

Shelley and jazz and lieder and love and hymn-tunes
  And day returns too soon;
We'll get drunk among the roses
  In the valley of the moon.
Give me an aphrodisiac, give me lotus,
  Give me the same again;
Make all the erotic poets of Rome and Ionia
  And Florence and Provence and Spain
Pay a tithe of their sugar to my potion
  And ferment my days
With the twang of Hawaii and the boom of the Congo;
  Let the old Muse loosen her stays
Or give me a new Muse with stockings and suspenders
209

And a smile like a cat,
With false eyelashes and finger-nails of carmine
  And dressed by Schiaparelli, with a pill-box hat.
Let the aces run riot round Brooklands,
  Let the tape-machines go drunk,
Turn on the purple spotlight, pull out the Vox Humana,
  Dig up somebody's body in a cloakroom trunk.
Give us sensations and then again sensations—
  Strip-tease, fireworks, all-in wrestling, gin;
Spend your capital, open your house and pawn your
    padlocks,
  Let the critical sense go out and the Roaring Boys
    come in.
Give me a houri but houris are too easy,
  Give me a nun;
We'll rape the angels off the golden reredos
  Before we're done.
Tiger-women and Lesbos, drums and entrails,
  And let the skies rotate,
We'll play roulette with the stars, we'll sit out drinking
  At the Hangman's Gate.
O look who comes here. I cannot see their faces
  Walking in file, slowly in file;
They have no shoes on their feet, the knobs of their ankles
  Catch the moonlight as they pass the stile
And cross the moor among the skeletons of bog-oak
  Following the track from the gallows back to the town;
Each has the end of a rope around his neck. I wonder
  Who let these men come back, who cut them down—
And now they reach the gate and line up opposite
  The neon lights on the medieval wall
And underneath the sky-signs

Each one takes his cowl and lets it fall
And we see their faces, each the same as the other,
    Men and women, each like a closed door,
But something about their faces is familiar;
    Where have we seen them before?
Was it the murderer on the nursery ceiling
    Or Judas Iscariot in the Field of Blood
Or someone at Gallipoli or in Flanders
    Caught in the end-all mud?
But take no notice of them, out with the ukulele,
    The saxophone and the dice;
They are sure to go away if we take no notice;
    Another round of drinks or make it twice.
That was a good one, tell us another, don't stop talking,
    Cap your stories; if
You haven't any new ones tell the old ones,
    Tell them as often as you like and perhaps those hor-
        rible stiff
People with blank faces that are yet familiar
    Won't be there when you look again, but don't
Look just yet, just give them time to vanish. I said to
        vanish;
    What do you mean—they won't?
Give us the songs of Harlem or Mitylene—
    Pearls in wine—
There can't be a hell unless there is a heaven
    And a devil would have to be divine
And there can't be such things one way or the other;
    That we know;
You can't step into the same river twice so there can't be
    Ghosts; thank God that rivers always flow.
Sufficient to the moment is the moment;

Past and future merely don't make sense
And yet I thought I had seen them . . .
    But *how,* if there is only a present tense?
Come on, boys, we aren't afraid of bogies,
    Give us another drink;
This little lady has a fetish,
    She goes to bed in mink.
This little pig went to market—
    Now I think you may look, I think the coast is clear.
Well, why don't you answer?
    I can't answer because they are still there.

xvi

Nightmare leaves fatigue:
    We envy men of action
Who sleep and wake, murder and intrigue
    Without being doubtful, without being haunted.
And I envy the intransigence of my own
    Countrymen who shoot to kill and never
See the victim's face become their own
    Or find his motive sabotage their motives.
So reading the memoirs of Maud Gonne,
    Daughter of an English mother and a soldier father,
I note how a single purpose can be founded on
    A jumble of opposites:
Dublin Castle, the vice-regal ball,
    The embassies of Europe,
Hatred scribbled on a wall,
    Gaols and revolvers.
And I remember, when I was little, the fear
    Bandied among the servants

212

That Casement would land at the pier
  With a sword and a horde of rebels;
And how we used to expect, at a later date,
  When the wind blew from the west, the noise of
    shooting
Starting in the evening at eight
  In Belfast in the York Street district;
And the voodoo of the Orange bands
  Drawing an iron net through darkest Ulster,
Flailing the limbo lands—
  The linen mills, the long wet grass, the ragged haw-
    thorn.
And one read black where the other read white, his hope
  The other man's damnation:
Up the Rebels, To Hell with the Pope,
  And God Save—as your prefer—the King or Ireland.
The land of scholars and saints:
  Scholars and saints my eye, the land of ambush,
Purblind manifestoes, never-ending complaints,
  The born martyr and the gallant ninny;
The grocer drunk with the drum,
  The land-owner shot in his bed, the angry voices
Piercing the broken fanlight in the slum,
  The shawled woman weeping at the garish altar.
Kathaleen ni Houlihan! Why
  Must a country, like a ship or a car, be always female,
Mother or sweetheart? A woman passing by,
  We did but see her passing.
Passing like a patch of sun on the rainy hill
  And yet we love her for ever and hate our neighbour
And each one in his will
  Binds his heirs to continuance of hatred.

Drums on the haycock, drums on the harvest, black
    Drums in the night shaking the windows:
King William is riding his white horse back
    To the Boyne on a banner.
Thousands of banners, thousands of white
    Horses, thousands of Williams
Waving thousands of swords and ready to fight
    Till the blue sea turns to orange.
Such was my country and I thought I was well
    Out of it, educated and domiciled in England,
Though yet her name keeps ringing like a bell
    In an under-water belfry.
Why do we like being Irish? Partly because
    It gives us an edge on the sentimental English
As members of a world that never was,
    Baptised with fairy water;
And partly because Ireland is small enough
    To be still thought of with a family feeling,
And because the waves are rough
    That split her from a more commercial culture;
And because one feels that here at least one can
    Do local work which is not at the world's mercy
And that on this tiny stage with luck a man
    Might see the end of one particular action.
It is self-deception of course;
    There is no immunity in this island either;
A cart that is drawn by somebody else's horse
    And carrying goods to somebody else's market.
The bombs in the turnip sack, the sniper from the roof,
    Griffith, Connolly, Collins, where have they brought
        us?
Ourselves alone! Let the round tower stand aloof

In a world of bursting mortar!
Let the school-children fumble their sums
  In a half-dead language;
Let the censor be busy on the books; pull down the
      Georgian slums;
  Let the games be played in Gaelic.
Let them grow beet-sugar; let them build
  A factory in every hamlet;
Let them pigeon-hole the souls of the killed
  Into sheep and goats, patriots and traitors.
And the North, where I was a boy,
  Is still the North, veneered with the grime of Glasgow,
Thousands of men whom nobody will employ
  Standing at the corners, coughing.
And the street-children play on the wet
  Pavement—hopscotch or marbles;
And each rich family boasts a sagging tennis-net
  On a spongy lawn beside a dripping shrubbery.
The smoking chimneys hint
  At prosperity round the corner
But they make their Ulster linen from foreign lint
  And the money that comes in goes out to make more
      money.
A city built upon mud;
  A culture built upon profit;
Free speech nipped in the bud,
  The minority always guilty.
Why should I want to go back
  To you, Ireland, my Ireland?
The blots on the page are so black
  That they cannot be covered with shamrock.
I hate your grandiose airs,

Your sob-stuff, your laugh and your swagger,
Your assumption that everyone cares
    Who is the king of your castle.
Castles are out of date,
    The tide flows round the children's sandy fancy;
Put up what flag you like, it is too late
    To save your soul with bunting.
Odi atque amo:
    Shall we cut this name on trees with a rusty dagger?
Her mountains are still blue, her rivers flow
    Bubbling over the boulders.
She is both a bore and a bitch;
    Better close the horizon,
Send her no more fantasy, no more longings which
    Are under a fatal tariff.
For common sense is the vogue
    And she gives her children neither sense nor money
Who slouch around the world with a gesture and a
        brogue
    And a faggot of useless memories.

xvii

From the second floor up, looking north, having breakfast
    I see the November sun at nine o'clock
Gild the fusty brickwork of rows on rows of houses
    Like animals asleep and breathing smoke
And savouring Well-being
    I light my first cigarette, grow giddy and blink,
Glad of this titillation, this innuendo,
    This make-believe of standing on a brink;
For all our trivial daily acts are altered

216

Into heroic or romantic make-believe
Of which we are hardly conscious—Who is it calls me
  When the cold draught picks my sleeve?
Or sneezing in the morning sunlight or smelling the bon-
      fire
  Over the webbed lawn and the naked cabbage plot?
Or stepping into a fresh-filled bath with strata
  Of cold water and hot?
We lie in the bath between tiled walls and under
  Ascending scrolls of steam
And feel the ego merge as the pores open
  And we lie in the bath and dream;
And responsibility dies and the thighs are happy
  And the body purrs like a cat
But this lagoon grows cold, we have to leave it, stepping
  On to a check rug on a cork mat.
The luxury life is only to be valued
  By those who are short of money or pressed for time
As the cinema gives the poor their Jacob's ladder
  For Cinderellas to climb.
And Plato was right to define the bodily pleasures
  As the pouring water into a hungry sieve
But wrong to ignore the rhythm which the intercrossing
  Coloured waters permanently give.
And Aristotle was right to posit the Alter Ego
  But wrong to make it only a halfway house:
Who could expect—or want—to be spiritually self-
      supporting,
  Eternal self-abuse?
Why not admit that other people are always
  Organic to the self, that a monologue
Is the death of language and that a single lion

Is less himself, or alive, than a dog and another dog?
Virtue going out of us always; the eyes grow weary
    With vision but it is vision builds the eye;
And in a sense the children kill their parents
    But do the parents die?
And the beloved destroys like fire or water
    But water scours and sculps and fire refines
And if you are going to read the testaments of cynics,
    You must read between the lines.
A point here and a point there: the current
    Jumps the gaps, the ego cannot live
Without becoming other for the Other
    Has got yourself to give.
And even the sense of taste provides communion
    With God as plant or beast;
The sea in fish, the field in a salad of endive,
    A sacramental feast.
The soul's long searchlight hankers for a body,
    The single body hungers for its kind,
The eye demands the light at the risk of blindness
    And the mind that did not doubt would not be mind
And discontent is eternal. In luxury or business,
    In family or sexual love, in purchases or prayers,
Our virtue is invested, the self put out at interest,
    The returns are never enough, the fact compares
So badly with the fancy yet fancy itself is only
    A divination of fact
And if we confine the world to the prophet's tripod
    The subjects of our prophecy contract.
Open the world wide, open the senses,
    Let the soul stretch its blind enormous arms,
There is vision in the fingers only needing waking,

Ready for light's alarms.
O light, terror of light, hoofs and ruthless
    Wheels of steel and brass
Dragging behind you lacerated captives
    Who also share your triumph as you pass.
Light which is time, belfry of booming sunlight,
    The ropes run up and down,
The whole town shakes with the peal of living people
    Who break and build the town.
Aristotle was right to think of man-in-action
    As the essential and really existent man
And man means men in action; try and confine your
    Self to yourself if you can.
Nothing is self-sufficient, pleasure implies hunger
    But hunger implies hope:
I cannot lie in this bath for ever, clouding
    The cooling water with rose geranium soap.
I cannot drug my life with the present moment;
    The present moment may rape—but all in vain—
The future, for the future remains a virgin
    Who must be tried again.

xviii

In the days that were early the music came easy
    On cradle and coffin, in the corn and the barn,
Songs for the reaping and spinning and only the shepherd
    Then as now was silent beside the tarn:
Cuffs of foam around the beer-brown water,
    Crinkled water and a mackerel sky;
It is all in the day's work—the grey stones and heather
    And the sheep that breed and break their legs and die.

The uplands now as then are fresh but in the valley
    Polluted rivers run—the Lethe and the Styx;
The soil is tired and the profit little and the hunchback
    Bobs on a carthorse round the sodden ricks.
Sing us no more idylls, no more pastorals,
    No more epics of the English earth;
The country is a dwindling annex to the factory,
    Squalid as an after-birth.
This England is tight and narrow, teeming with un-
        wanted
    Children who are so many, each is alone;
Niobe and her children
    Stand beneath the smokestack turned to stone.
And still the church-bells brag above the empty churches
    And the Union Jack
Thumps the wind above the law-courts and the barracks
    And in the allotments the black
Scarecrow holds a fort of grimy heads of cabbage
    Besieged by grimy birds
Like a hack politician fighting the winged aggressor
    With yesterday's magic coat of ragged words.
Things were different when men felt their programme
    In the bones and pulse, not only in the brain,
Born to a trade, a belief, a set of affections;
    That instinct for belief may sprout again,
There are some who never lost it
    And some who foster or force it into growth
But most of us lack the right discontent, contented
    Merely to cavil. Spiritual sloth
Creeps like lichen or ivy over the hinges
    Of the doors which never move;
We cannot even remember who is behind them

Nor even, soon, shall have the chance to prove
If anyone at all is behind them—
    The Sleeping Beauty or the Holy Ghost
Or the greatest happiness of the greatest number;
    All we can do at most
Is press an anxious ear against the keyhole
    To hear the Future breathing; softly tread
In the outer porch beneath the marble volutes—
    Who knows if God, as Nietzsche said, is dead?
There is straw to lay in the streets; call the hunchback,
    The gentleman farmer, the village idiot, the Shrop-
        shire Lad,
To insulate us if they can with coma
    Before we all go mad.
What shall we pray for, Lord? Whom shall we pray to?
    Shall we give like decadent Athens the benefit of the
        doubt
To the Unknown God or smugly pantheistic
    Assume that God is everywhere round about?
But if we assume such a God, then who the devil
    Are these with empty stomachs or empty smiles?
The blind man's stick goes tapping on the pavement
    For endless glittering miles
Beneath the standard lights; the paralytic winding
    His barrel-organ sprays the passers-by
With April music; the many-ribboned hero
    With half a lung or a leg waits his turn to die.
God forbid an Indian acquiescence,
    The apotheosis of the *status quo;*
If everything that happens happens according
    To the nature and wish of God, then God must go:
Lay your straw in the streets and go about your business

An inch at a time, an inch at a time,
We have not even an hour to spend repenting
    Our sins; the quarters chime
And every minute is its own alarum clock
    And what we are about to do
Is of vastly more importance
    Than what we have done or not done hitherto.
It is December now, the trees are naked
    As the three crosses on the hill;
Through the white fog the face of the orange sun is
        cryptic
    Like a lawyer making the year's will.
The year has little to show, will leave a heavy
    Overdraft to its heir;
Shall we try to meet the deficit or passing
    By on the other side continue *laissez-faire?*
International betrayals, public murder,
    The devil quoting scripture, the traitor, the coward,
        the thug
Eating dinner in the name of peace and progress,
    The doped public sucking a dry dug;
Official recognition of rape, revival of the ghetto
    And free speech gagged and free
Energy scrapped and dropped like surplus herring
    Back into the barren sea;
Brains and beauty festering in exile,
    The shadow of bars
Falling across each page, each field, each raddled sunset,
    The alien lawn and the pool of nenuphars;
And hordes of homeless poor running the gauntlet
    In hostile city streets of white and violet lamps
Whose flight is without a terminus but better

Than the repose of concentration camps.
Come over, they said, into Macedonia and help us
   But the chance is gone;
Now we must help ourselves, we can leave the vulture
   To pick the corpses clean in Macedon.
No wonder many would renounce their birthright,
   The responsibility of moral choice,
And sit with a mess of pottage taking orders
   Out of a square box from a mad voice—
Lies on the air endlessly repeated
   Turning the air to fog,
Blanket on blanket of lie, no room to breathe or fidget
   And nobody to jog
Your elbow and say 'Up there the sun is rising;
   Take it on trust, the sun will always shine.'
The sun may shine no doubt but how many people
   Will see it with their eyes in 1939?
Yes, the earlier days had their music,
   We have some still to-day,
But the orchestra is due for the bonfire
   If things go on this way.
Still there are still the seeds of energy and choice
   Still alive even if forbidden, hidden,
And while a man has voice
   He may recover music.

xix

The pigeons riddle the London air,
   The shutter slides from the chain-store window,
The frock-coat statue stands in the square
   Caring for no one, caring for no one.

The night-shift men go home to bed,
    The kettle sings and the bacon sizzles;
Some are hungry and some are dead—
    A wistful face in a faded photo.
Under the stairs is a khaki cap;
    That was Dad's, Dad was a plumber—
You hear that dripping tap?
    He'd have had it right in no time.
No time now; Dad is dead,
    He left me five months gone or over;
Tam cari capitis, for such a well-loved head
    What shame in tears, what limit?
It is the child I mean,
    Born prematurely, strangled;
Dad was off the scene,
    He would have made no difference.
The stretchers run from ward to ward,
    The telephone rings in empty houses,
The torn shirt soaks on the scrubbing board,
    O what a busy morning.
Baby Croesus crawls in a pen
    With alphabetical bricks and biscuits;
The doll-dumb file of sandwichmen
    Carry lies from gutter to gutter.
The curate buys his ounce of shag,
    The typist tints her nails with coral,
The housewife with her shopping bag
    Watches the cleaver catch the naked
New Zealand sheep between the legs—
    What price now New Zealand?
The cocker spaniel sits and begs
    With eyes like a waif on the movies.

O what a busy morning,
 Engines start with a roar,
All the wires are buzzing,
 The tape-machines vomit on the floor.
And I feel that my mind once again is open;
 She has gone away who stood in the way so long,
The hypnosis is over and no one
 Calls encore to the song.
When we are out of love, how were we ever in it?
 Where are the mountains and the mountain skies,
That heady air instinct with
 A strange sincerity which winged our lies?
The peaks have fallen in like dropping pastry:
 Now I could see her come
Around the corner without the pulse responding,
 The flowery orator in the heart is dumb,
His bag of tricks is empty, his over-statements,
 Those rainbow bubbles, have burst:
When we meet, she need not feel embarrassed,
 The agent of my dreams has done his worst
And has no orders from me to mix his phrases rich,
 To make the air a carpet
For her to walk on; I only wonder which
 Day, which hour, I found this freedom.
But freedom is not so exciting,
 We prefer to be drawn
In the rush of the stars as they circle—
 A traffic that ends with dawn.
Now I am free of the stars
 And the word 'love' makes no sense, this history is
  almost
Ripe for the mind's museum—broken jars

That once held wine or perfume.
Yet looking at their elegance on the stands
    I feel a certain pride that only lately
(And yet so long ago) I held them in my hands
    While they were full and fragrant.
So on this busy morning I hope, my dear,
    That you are also busy
With the mixed vintage of another year;
    Pain, they say, is always twin to pleasure.
Better to have these twins
    Than no children at all, very much better
To act for good and bad than have no sins
    And take no action either.
You were my blizzard who had been my bed
    But taking the whole series of blight and blossom
I would not choose a simpler crop instead;
    Thank you, my dear—dear against my judgment.

xx

Nelson stands on a black pillar,
    The electric signs go off and on—
Distilleries and life insurance companies—
    The traffic circles, coming and gone,
Past the National Gallery closed and silent
    Where in their frames
Other worlds persist, the passions of the artist
    Caught like frozen flames:
The Primitives distilling from the cruel
    Legend a faith that is almost debonair,
Sebastian calmly waiting the next arrow,
    The crucifixion in the candid air:

226

And Venice lolling in wealth for ever under glass,
    Pearls in her hair, panther and velvet:
And the rococo picnic on the grass
    With wine and lutes and banter:
And the still life proclaiming with aplomb
    The self-content of bread or fruit or vases
And personality like a silent bomb
    Lurking in the formal portrait.
Here every day the visitors walk slowly
    Rocking along the parquet as if on a ship's deck
Feeling a vague affinity with the pictures
    Yet wary of these waves which gently peck
The side of the boat in passing; they are anxious
    To end the voyage, to land in their own time;
The sea of the past glimmers with white horses,
    A paradigm
Of life's successions, treacheries, recessions;
    The unfounded confidence of the dead affronts
Our own system of values
    Like airmen doing their stunts
Over our private garden; these arrogant Old Masters
    Swoop and loop and lance us with a quick
Shadow; we only want to cultivate our garden,
    Not for us the virtuoso, slick
Tricks of the airy region,
    For our part our feet are on the ground,
They should not be allowed to fly so low above us,
    Their premises are unsound
And history has refuted them and yet
    They cast their shadows on us like aspersions;
Propellers and white horses,
    Movement, movement, can we never forget

The movements of the past which should be dead?
   The mind of Socrates still clicks like scissors
And Christ who should lie quiet in the garden
   Flowered in flame instead.

.   .   .   .   .

A week to Christmas, cards of snow and holly,
   Gimcracks in the shops,
Wishes and memories wrapped in tissue paper,
   Trinkets, gadgets and lollipops
And as if through coloured glasses
   We remember our childhood's thrill
Waking in the morning to the rustling of paper,
   The eiderdown heaped in a hill
Of wogs and dogs and bears and bricks and apples
   And the feeling that Christmas Day
Was a coral island in time where we land and eat our
      lotus
   But where we can never stay.
There was a star in the East, the magi in their turbans
   Brought their luxury toys
In homage to a child born to capsize their values
   And wreck their equipoise.
A smell of hay like peace in the dark stable—
   Not peace however but a sword
To cut the Gordian knot of logical self-interest,
   The fool-proof golden cord;
For Christ walked in where no philosopher treads
   But armed with more than folly,
Making the smooth place rough and knocking the heads
   Of Church and State together.
In honour of whom we have taken over the pagan

Saturnalia for our annual treat
Letting the belly have its say, ignoring
   The spirit while we eat.
And Conscience still goes crying through the desert
   With sackcloth round his loins:
A week to Christmas—hark the herald angels
   Beg for copper coins.

                    xxi

And when we clear away
   All this debris of day-by-day experience,
What comes out to light, what is there of value
   Lasting from day to day?
I sit in my room in comfort
   Looking at enormous flowers—
Equipment purchased with my working hours,
   A daily mint of perishable petals.
The figures of the dance repeat
   The unending cycle of making and spending money,
Eating our daily bread in order to earn it
   And earning in order to eat.
And is that all the story,
   The mainspring and the plot,
Or merely a mechanism without which not
   Any story could be written?
Sine qua non!
   Sine qua non indeed, we cannot ever
Live by soul alone; the soul without the stomach
   Would find its glory gone.
But the total cause outruns the mere condition,
   There is more to it than that;

Life would be (as it often seems) flat
    If it were merely a matter of not dying.
For each individual then
    Would be fighting a losing battle
But with life as collective creation
    The rout is rallied, the battle begins again.
Only give us the courage of our instinct,
    The will to truth and love's initiative,
Then we could hope to live
    A life beyond the self but self-completing.
And, as the emperor said, What is the use
    Of the minor loyalty—'Dear city of Cecrops,'
Unless we have also the wider franchise, can answer
    'Dear city of Zeus'?
And so when the many regrets
    Trouble us for the many lost affections,
Let us take the wider view before we count them
    Hopelessly bad debts.
For Cecrops has his rights as Zeus has his
    And every tree is a tree of branches
And every wood is a wood of trees growing
    And what has been contributes to what is.
So I am glad to have known them,
    The people or events apparently withdrawn;
The world is round and there is always dawn
    Undeniably somewhere.
'Praised be thou, O Lord, for our brother the sun'
    Said the grey saint, laving his eyes in colour;
Who creates and destroys for ever
    And his cycle is never done.
In this room chrysanthemums and dahlias
    Like brandy hit the heart; the fire,

A small wild animal, furthers its desire
  Consuming fuel, self-consuming.
And flames are the clearest cut
  Of shapes and the most transient:
O fire, my spendthrift,
  May I spend like you, as reckless but
Giving as good return—burn the silent
  Into running sound, deride the dark
And jump to glory from a single spark
  And purge the world and warm it.
The room grows cold, the flicker fades,
  The sinking ashes whisper, the fickle
Eye forgets but later will remember
  The radiant cavalcades.
The smoke has gone from the chimney,
  The water has flowed away under the bridge,
The silhouetted lovers have left the ridge,
  The flower has closed its calyx.
The crow's-feet have come to stay,
  The jokes no longer amuse, the palate
Rejects milk chocolate and Benedictine—
  Yesterday and the day before yesterday.
But oh, not now my love, but oh my friend,
  Can you not take it merely on trust that life is
The only thing worth living and that dying
  Had better be left to take care of itself in the end?
To have been born is in itself a triumph
  Among all that waste of sperm
And it is gratitude to wait the proper term
  Or, if not gratitude, duty.
I know that you think these phrases highfalutin
  And, when not happy, see no claim or use

For staying alive; the quiet hands seduce
    Of the god who is god of nothing.
And while I sympathise
    With the wish to quit, to make the great refusal,
I feel that such a defeat is also treason,
    That deaths like these are lies.
A fire should be left burning
    Till it burns itself out:
We shan't have another chance to dance and shout
    Once the flames are silent.

xxii

December the nineteenth: over the black roofs
    And the one black paint-brush poplar
The white steam rises and deploys in puffs
    From the house-hidden railway, a northern
Geyser erupting in a land of lava,
    But white can be still whiter for now
The dun air starts to jig with specks that circle
    Like microbes under a lens; this is the first snow;
And soon the specks are feathers blandly sidling
    Inconsequent as the fancies of young girls
And the air has filled like a dance-hall,
    A waltz of white dresses and strings of pearls.
And the papers declare the snow has come to stay,
    A new upholstery on roof and garden
Refining, lining, underlining the day,
    And the sombre laurels break parole and blossom
In enormous clumps of peonies; and the cars
    Turn animal, moving slowly
In their white fur like bears,

232

And the white trees fade into the hill behind them
As niggers' faces fade in a dark background,
   Our London world
Grown all of a piece and peaceful like the Arctic,
   The sums all cancelled out and the flags furled.
At night we sleep behind stockades of frost,
   Nothing alive in the streets to run the gauntlet
Of this unworldly cold except the lost
   Wisps of steam from the gratings of the sewers.
It is holiday time, time for the morning snack,
   Time to be leaving the country:
I have taken my ticket south, I will not look back,
   The pipes may burst for all I care, the gutter
Dribble with dirty snow, the Christmas party
   Be ruined by catarrh;
Let us flee this country and leave its complications
   Exactly where they (the devil take them) are.
So Dover to Dunkerque:
   The Land of Cockayne begins across the Channel;
The hooter cries to hell with the year's work,
   The snowflakes flirt with the steam of the steamer.
But the train in France is cold, the window
   Frosted with patterns of stars and fern,
And when we scrape a peephole on the window
   There is nothing new to learn;
Nothing but snow and snow all the way to Paris,
   No roast pigs walk this way
And any snatched half-hour of self-indulgence
   Is an intercalary day.
Sweet, my love, my dear, whoever you are or were,
   I need your company on this excursion
For, where there is the luxury of leisure, there

There should also be the luxury of women.
I do not need you on my daily job
    Nor yet on any spiritual adventure,
Not when I earn my keep but when I rob
    Time of his growth of tinsel:
No longer thinking you or any other
    Essential to my life—soul-mate or dual star;
All I want is an elegant and witty playmate
    At the perfume counter or the cocktail bar.
So here where tourist values are the only
    Values, where we pretend
That eating and drinking are more important than
        thinking
    And looking at things than action and a casual friend
Than a colleague and that work is a dull convenience
    Designed to provide
Money to spend on amusement and that amusement
    Is an eternal bride
Who will never sink to the level of a wife, that gossip
    Is the characteristic of art
And that the sensible man must keep his aesthetic
    And his moral standards apart—
Here, where we think all this, I need you badly,
    Whatever your name or age or the colour of your hair;
I need your surface company (what happens
    Below the surface is my own affair).
And I feel a certain pleasurable nostalgia
    In sitting alone, drinking, wondering if you
Will suddenly thread your way among these vulcanite
        tables
    To a mutually unsuspected rendezvous

Among these banal women with feathers in their hats and
    halos
    Of evanescent veils
And these bald-at-thirty Englishmen whose polished
    Foreheads are the tombs of record sales;
Where alcohol, anchovies and shimmying street-lamps
    Knock the stolid almanac cock-a-hoop,
Where reason drowns and the senses
    Foam, flame, tingle and loop the loop.
And striking red or green matches to light these loose
    Cigarettes of black tobacco I need you badly—
The age-old woman apt for all misuse
    Whose soul is out of the picture.
How I enjoy this bout of cynical self-indulgence,
    Of glittering and hard-boiled make-believe;
The cynic is a creature of over-statements
    But an over-statement is something to achieve.
And how (with a grain of salt) I enjoy hating
    The world to which for ever I belong,
This hatred, this escape, being equally factitious—
    A passing song.
For I cannot stay in Paris
    And, if I did, no doubt I should soon be bored
For what I see is not the intimate city
    But the brittle dance of lights in the Place de la Con-
    corde.
So much for Christmas: I must go further south
    To see the New Year in on hungry faces
But where the hungry mouth
    Refuses to deny the heart's allegiance.
Look: the road winds up among the prickly vineyards

235

And naked winter trees;
Over there are pain and pride beyond the snow-lit
Sharp annunciation of the Pyrenees.

xxiii

The road ran downhill into Spain,
The wind blew fresh on bamboo grasses,
The white plane-trees were bone-naked
And the issues plain:
We have come to a place in space where shortly
All of us may be forced to camp in time:
The slender searchlights climb,
Our sins will find us out, even our sins of omission.
When I reached the town it was dark,
No lights in the streets but two and a half millions
Of people in circulation
Condemned like the beasts in the ark
With nothing but water around them:
Will there ever be a green tree or a rock that is dry?
The shops are empty and in Barceloneta the eye-
Sockets of the houses are empty.
But still they manage to laugh
Though they have no eggs, no milk, no fish, no fruit,
no tobacco, no butter
Though they live upon lentils and sleep in the Metro,
Though the old order is gone and the golden calf
Of Catalan industry shattered;
The human values remain, purged in the fire,
And it appears that every man's desire

Is life rather than victuals.
Life being more, it seems, than merely the bare
　　Permission to keep alive and receive orders,
Humanity being more than a mechanism
　　To be oiled and greased and for ever unaware
Of the work it is turning out, of why the wheels keep
　　　　turning;
　　Here at least the soul has found its voice
Though not indeed by choice;
　　The cost was heavy.
They breathe the air of war and yet the tension
　　Admits, beside the slogans it evokes,
An interest in philately or pelota
　　Or private jokes.
And the sirens cry in the dark morning
　　And the lights go out and the town is still
And the sky is pregnant with ill-will
　　And the bombs come foxing the fated victim.
As pretty as a Guy Fawkes show—
　　Silver sprays and tracer bullets—
And in the pauses of destruction
　　The cocks in the centre of the town crow.
The cocks crow in Barcelona
　　Where clocks are few to strike the hour;
Is it the heart's reveille or the sour
　　Reproach of Simon Peter?
The year has come to an end,
　　Time for resolutions, for stock-taking;
Felice Nuevo Año!
　　May God, if there is one, send
As much courage again and greater vision

And resolve the antinomies in which we live
Where man must be either safe because he is negative
　　Or free on the edge of a razor.
Give those who are gentle strength,
　　Give those who are strong a generous imagination,
And make their half-truth true and let the crooked
　　Footpath find its parent road at length.
I admit that for myself I cannot straighten
　　My broken rambling track
Which reaches so irregularly back
　　To burning cities and rifled rose-bushes
And cairns and lonely farms
　　Where no one lives, makes love or begets children,
All my heredity and my upbringing
　　Having brought me only to the Present's arms—
The arms not of a mistress but of a wrestler,
　　Of a God who straddles over the night sky;
No wonder Jacob halted on his thigh—
　　The price of a drawn battle.
For never to begin
　　Anything new because we know there is nothing
New, is an academic sophistry—
　　The original sin.
I have already had friends
　　Among things and hours and people
But taking them one by one—odd hours and passing
　　　　people;
　　Now I must make amends
And try to correlate event with instinct
　　And me with you or you and you with all,
No longer think of time as a waterfall
　　Abstracted from a river.

I have loved defeat and sloth,
    The tawdry halo of the idle martyr;
I have thrown away the roots of will and conscience,
    Now I must look for both,
Not any longer act among the cushions
    The Dying Gaul;
Soon or late the delights of self-pity must pall
    And the fun of cursing the wicked
World into which we were born
    And the cynical admission of frustration
('Our loves are not full measure,
    There are blight and rooks on the corn').
Rather for any measure so far given
    Let us be glad
Nor wait on purpose to be wisely sad
    When doing nothing we find we have gained nothing.
For here and now the new valkyries ride
    The Spanish constellations
As over the Plaza Cataluña
    Orion lolls on his side;
Droning over from Majorca
    To maim or blind or kill
The bearers of the living will,
    The stubborn heirs of freedom
Whose matter-of-fact faith and courage shame
    Our niggling equivocations—
We who play for safety,
    A safety only in name.
Whereas these people contain truth, whatever
    Their nominal façade.
Listen: a whirr, a challenge, an aubade—
    It is the cock crowing in Barcelona.

Sleep, my body, sleep, my ghost,
   Sleep, my parents and grandparents,
And all those I have loved most:
   One man's coffin is another's cradle.
Sleep, my past and all my sins,
   In distant snow or dried roses
Under the moon for night's cocoon will open
   When day begins.
Sleep, my fathers, in your graves
   On upland bogland under heather;
What the wind scatters the wind saves,
   A sapling springs in a new country.
Time is a country, the present moment
   A spotlight roving round the scene;
We need not chase the spotlight,
   The future is the bride of what has been.
Sleep, my fancies and my wishes,
   Sleep a little and wake strong,
The same but different and take my blessing—
   A cradle-song.
And sleep, my various and conflicting
   Selves I have so long endured,
Sleep in Asclepius' temple
   And wake cured.
And you with whom I shared an idyll
   Five years long,
Sleep beyond the Atlantic
   And wake to a glitter of dew and to bird-song.
And you whose eyes are blue, whose ways are foam,
   Sleep quiet and smiling

And do not hanker
    For a perfection which can never come.
And you whose minutes patter
    To crowd the social hours,
Curl up easy in a placid corner
    And let your thoughts close in like flowers.
And you, who work for Christ, and you, as eager
    For a better life, humanist, atheist,
And you, devoted to a cause, and you, to a family,
    Sleep and may your beliefs and zeal persist.
Sleep quietly, Marx and Freud,
    The figure-heads of our transition.
Cagney, Lombard, Bing and Garbo,
    Sleep in your world of celluloid.
Sleep now also, monk and satyr,
    Cease your wrangling for a night.
Sleep, my brain, and sleep, my senses,
    Sleep, my hunger and my spite.
Sleep, recruits to the evil army,
    Who, for so long misunderstood,
Took to the gun to kill your sorrow;
    Sleep and be damned and wake up good.
While we sleep, what shall we dream?
    Of Tir nan Og or South Sea islands,
Of a land where all the milk is cream
    And all the girls are willing?
Or shall our dream be earnest of the real
    Future when we wake,
Design a home, a factory, a fortress
    Which, though with effort, we can really make?
What is it we want really?
    For what end and how?

If it is something feasible, obtainable,
    Let us dream it now,
And pray for a possible land
    Not of sleep-walkers, not of angry puppets,
But where both heart and brain can understand
    The movements of our fellows;
Where life is a choice of instruments and none
    Is debarred his natural music,
Where the waters of life are free of the ice-blockade of
        hunger
    And thought is free as the sun,
Where the altars of sheer power and mere profit
    Have fallen to disuse,
Where nobody sees the use
    Of buying money and blood at the cost of blood and
        money,
Where the individual, no longer squandered
    In self-assertion, works with the rest, endowed
With the split vision of a juggler and the quick lock of a
        taxi,
    Where the people are more than a crowd.
So sleep in hope of this—but only for a little;
    Your hope must wake
While the choice is yours to make,
    The mortgage not foreclosed, the offer open.
Sleep serene, avoid the backward
    Glance; go forward, dreams, and do not halt
(Behind you in the desert stands a token
    Of doubt—a pillar of salt).
Sleep, the past, and wake, the future,
    And walk out promptly through the open door;
But you, my coward doubts, may go on sleeping,

You need not wake again—not any more.
The New Year comes with bombs, it is too late
    To dose the dead with honourable intentions:
If you have honour to spare, employ it on the living;
    The dead are dead as 1938.
Sleep to the noise of running water
    To-morrow to be crossed, however deep;
This is no river of the dead or Lethe,
    To-night we sleep
On the banks of Rubicon—the die is cast;
    There will be time to audit
The accounts later, there will be sunlight later
    And the equation will come out at last.

VII

POEMS: 1939–1940

PROGNOSIS

Good-bye, Winter,
The days are getting longer,
The tea-leaf in the teacup
Is herald of a stranger.

Will he bring me business
Or will he bring me gladness
Or will he come for cure
Of his own sickness?

With a pedlar's burden
Walking up the garden
Will he come to beg
Or will he come to bargain?

Will he come to pester,
To cringe or to bluster,
A promise in his palm
Or a gun in his holster?

Will his name be John
Or will his name be Jonah
Crying to repent
On the Island of Iona?

Will his name be Jason
Looking for a seaman
Or a mad crusader
Without rhyme or reason?

What will be his message—
War or work or marriage?
News as new as dawn
Or an old adage?

Will he give a champion
Answer to my question
Or will his words be dark
And his ways evasion?

Will his name be Love
And all his talk be crazy?
Or will his name be Death
And his message easy?

                              [Spring, 1939]

STYLITE

The saint on the pillar stands,
The pillar is alone,
He has stood so long
That he himself is stone;
Only his eyes
Range across the sand
Where no one ever comes
And the world is banned.

Then his eyes close,
He stands in his sleep,
Round his neck there comes
The conscience of a rope,
248

And the hangman counting
Counting to ten—
At nine he finds
He has eyes again.

The saint on the pillar stands,
The pillars are two,
A young man opposite
Stands in the blue,
A white Greek god,
Confident, with curled
Hair above the groin
And his eyes on the world.

[March, 1940]

ENTIRELY

If we could get the hang of it entirely
    It would take too long;
All we know is the splash of words in passing
    And falling twigs of song,
And when we try to eavesdrop on the great
    Presences it is rarely
That by a stroke of luck we can appropriate
    Even a phrase entirely.

If we could find our happiness entirely
    In somebody else's arms
We should not fear the spears of the spring nor the city's
    Yammering fire alarms

But, as it is, the spears each year go through
    Our flesh and almost hourly
Bell or siren banishes the blue
    Eyes of Love entirely.

And if the world were black or white entirely
    And all the charts were plain
Instead of a mad weir of tigerish waters,
    A prism of delight and pain,
We might be surer where we wished to go
    Or again we might be merely
Bored but in brute reality there is no
    Road that is right entirely.

                                        [March, 1940]

PLANT AND PHANTOM

Man: a flutter of pages,
Leaves in the Sibyl's cave,
Shadow changing from dawn to twilight,
Murmuration of corn in the wind,
A shaking of hands with hallucinations,
Hobnobbing with ghosts, a pump of blood,
Mirage, a spider dangling
Over chaos and man a chaos.

Who cheats the pawky Fates
By what he does, not is,
By what he makes, imposing
On flux an architectonic—

Cone of marble, calyx of ice,
Spandrel and buttress, iron
Loops across the void,
Stepping stones in the random.

Man: a dance of midges,
Gold glass in the sunlight,
Prattle of water, palaver
Of starlings in a disused
Chimney, a gimcrack castle,
Seaweed tugging the rocks,
Guttering candles, the Northern
Lights and the Seventh Wave.

Whose life is a bluff, professing
To follow the laws of Nature,
In fact a revolt, a mad
Conspiracy and usurpation,
Smuggling over the frontier
Of fact a sense of value,
Metabolism of death,
Re-orchestration of world.

Man: a riot of banners,
Bulge in the wind, a prism,
Organ-pipes in the sunset,
Orgy of brains and glands,
Thunder-crackle and the bounce of hail,
Wink of wings and fog's delusion,
A rampant martyr, a midnight
Echo, a forest fire.

Who felt with his hands in empty
Air for the Word and did not
Find it but felt the aura,
Dew on the skin, could not forget it.
Ever since has fumbled, intrigued,
Clambered behind and beyond, and learnt
Words of blessing and cursing, hoping
To find in the end the Word Itself.

[September, 1940]

THE BRITISH MUSEUM READING ROOM

Under the hive-like dome the stooping haunted readers
Go up and down the alleys, tap the cells of knowledge—
   Honey and wax, the accumulation of years—
Some on commission, some for the love of learning,
Some because they have nothing better to do
Or because they hope these walls of books will deaden
   The drumming of the demon in their ears.

Cranks, hacks, poverty-stricken scholars,
In pince-nez, period hats or romantic beards
   And cherishing their hobby or their doom
Some are too much alive and some are asleep
Hanging like bats in a world of inverted values,
Folded up in themselves in a world which is safe and
     silent:
   This is the British Museum Reading Room.

Out on the steps in the sun the pigeons are courting,
Puffing their ruffs and sweeping their tails or taking
   A sun-bath at their ease
And under the totem poles—the ancient terror—
Between the enormous fluted Ionic columns
There seeps from heavily jowled or hawk-like foreign
      faces
   The guttural sorrow of the refugees.
                                        [July, 1939]

LONDON RAIN

The rain of London pimples
The ebony street with white
And the neon-lamps of London
Stain the canals of night
And the park becomes a jungle
In the alchemy of night.

My wishes turn to violent
Horses black as coal—
The randy mares of fancy,
The stallions of the soul—
Eager to take the fences
That fence about my soul.

Across the countless chimneys
The horses ride and across
The country to the channel

Where warning beacons toss,
To a place where God and No-God
Play at pitch and toss.

Whichever wins I am happy
For God will give me bliss
But No-God will absolve me
From all I do amiss
And I need not suffer conscience
If the world was made amiss.

Under God we can reckon
On pardon when we fall
But if we are under No-God
Nothing will matter at all,
Adultery and murder
Will count for nothing at all.

So reinforced by logic
As having nothing to lose
My lust goes riding horseback
To ravish where I choose,
To burgle all the turrets
Of beauty as I choose.

But now the rain gives over
Its dance upon the town,
Logic and lust together
Come dimly tumbling down,
And neither God nor No-God
Is either up or down.

The argument was wilful,
The alternatives untrue,
We need no metaphysics
To sanction what we do
Or to muffle us in comfort
From what we did not do.

Whether the living river
Began in bog or lake,
The world is what was given,
The world is what we make.
And we only can discover
Life in the life we make.

So let the water sizzle
Upon the gleaming slates,
There will be sunshine after
When the rain abates,
And rain returning duly
When the sun abates.

My wishes now come homeward,
Their gallopings in vain,
Logic and lust are quiet
And again it starts to rain
And falling asleep I listen
To the falling London rain.

[July, 1939]

PRIMROSE HILL

They cut the trees away:
By day the lean guns leer
Across their concrete walls;
The evening falls
On four guns tucked in bed.

The top of the hill is bare
But the trees beneath it stretch
Through Regent's Park and reach
A rim of jewelled lights—
The music of the fair.

And the wind gets up and blows
The lamps between the trees
And all the leaves are waves
And the top of Primrose Hill
A raft on stormy seas.

Some day the raft will lift
Upon a larger swell
And the evil sirens call
And the searchlights quest and shift
And out of the Milky Way
The impartial bombs will fall.

[June, 1939]

MEN OF GOOD WILL

We stand convicted
Votaries of the topical and transitory,
We put in words what is topical and transitory,
Anyone can detect it.

You need not tell us what we know—
That our words are slight, trite and ineffectual;
Our life itself is slight and ineffectual,
We have told it so.

That is a half truth
But it is the patent half, the rest is mere conjecture,
We leave a prayer a day on the altar of conjecture
Hoping for growth.

But we shall not pretend
To have met any vision on the road to Damascus;
We may, or may not, be on the road to Damascus—
We shall know in the end.

Meanwhile, meanwhile only
We take what we can, we talk with whom we can
And catch with all our hands at anything at all that can
Prevent us feeling lonely.

[November, 1939]

PICTURE GALLERIES

Strolling, guidebook in hand, along the varnished par-
    quet
We meet the calm of opium in the long galleries,
    An under-water dream, a closed
World whose people live in frames, the flames of their
    self-centred
Affections frozen, the bread and fruit on their tables fos-
    sil,
    A curfew—once for all—imposed
Upon their might-be wanderings; their might-be appli-
    cations
    For resurrection in advance refused.

Yet were violent monsters, whom the retiring ocean
Left embedded in sandstone: Michelangelo's tortured
    Urge to God, Greco's fugue of fire,
Goya's sleight-of-hand that fooled his patrons, Blake's
    ingenuous
Usurpation of reality, Daumier watching the bubbles
    rising
    From mouths of the drowned; panic, desire,
Fantasy, joy of the earth—the rhythm lurks in the canvas,
    sometimes
    If we look long, is more than we can bear.

Or viewed as history they remind us of what we always
Would rather forget—that what we are or prefer is con-
    ditioned
    By circumstances, that evil and good

Are relative to ourselves who are creatures of period;
        seeing
That what, for instance, Zurbaran found in his Carthu-
        sians
    Serene in white, with rope girdle and hood,
Lautrec discovered in brothel and circus; the answers
        were even
    Even though we today may find them odd.

A curator rings a bell: tourists, connoisseurs and loafers,
School-children with their teachers, hustle for the door,
        many
    Of their faces tired or showing relief
At leaving a silence which was a crowd of voices, the
        language
Like that of a paralytic hard to follow; they descend the
        staircase
    Into the open air, a sheaf
Of inklings fluttering in their minds, and now even the
        open
    Air is half-articulate and unsafe.

                                        [August, 1940]

THE COMING OF WAR

(Dublin, Cushendun, the West of Ireland, and back.)

I

Dublin

Grey brick upon brick,
Declamatory bronze
On sombre pedestals—
O'Connell, Grattan, Moore—
And the brewery tugs and the swans
On the balustraded stream
And the bare bones of a fanlight
Over a hungry door
And the air soft on the cheek
And porter running from the taps
With a head of yellow cream
And Nelson on his pillar
Watching his world collapse.

This was never my town,
I was not born nor bred
Nor schooled here and she will not
Have me alive or dead
But yet she holds my mind
With her seedy elegance,
With her gentle veils of rain
And all her ghosts that walk
And all that hide behind

Her Regency façades—
The catcalls and the pain,
The glamour of her squalor,
The bravado of her talk.

The lights jig in the river
With a concertina movement
And the sun comes up in the morning
Like barley-sugar on the water
And the mist on the Wicklow hills
Is close, as close
As the peasantry were to the landlord,
As the Irish to the Anglo-Irish,
As the killer is close one moment
To the man he kills,
Or as the moment itself
Is close to the next moment.

She is not an Irish town
And she is not English,
Historic with guns and vermin
And the cold renown
Of a fragment of Church latin,
Of an oratorical phrase.
But O the days are soft,
Soft enough to forget
The lesson better learnt,
The bullet on the wet
Streets, the crooked deal,
The steel behind the laugh,
The Four Courts burnt.

Fort of the Dane,
Garrison of the Saxon,
Augustan capital
Of a Gaelic nation,
Appropriating all
The alien brought,
You give me time for thought
And by a juggler's trick
You poise the toppling hour—
O greyness run to flower,
Grey stone, grey water
And brick upon grey brick.

II

Cushendun

Fuchsia and ragweed and the distant hills
Made as it were out of clouds and sea:
All night the bay is plashing and the moon
   Marks the break of the waves.

Limestone and basalt and a whitewashed house
With passages of great stone flags
And a walled garden with plums on the wall
   And a bird piping in the night.

Forgetfulness: brass lamps and copper jugs
And home-made bread and the smell of turf or flax
And the air a glove and the water lathering easy
   And convolvulus in the hedge.

Only in the dark green room beside the fire
With the curtains drawn against the winds and waves
There is a little box with a well-bred voice:
    What a place to talk of War.

III

County Sligo

In Sligo the country was soft; there were turkeys
    Gobbling under sycamore trees
And the shadows of clouds on the mountains moving
    Like browsing cattle at ease.

And little distant fields were sprigged with haycocks
    And splashed against a white
Roadside cottage a welter of nasturtium
    Deluging the sight,

And pullets pecking the flies from around the eyes of
        heifers
    Sitting in farmyard mud
Among hydrangeas and the falling ear-rings
    Of fuchsias red as blood.

But in Mayo the tumbledown walls went leap-frog
    Over the moors,
The sugar and salt in the pubs were damp in the casters
    And the water was brown as beer upon the shores

263

Of desolate loughs, and stumps of hoary bog-oak
  Stuck up here and there
And as the twilight filtered on the heather
  Water-music filled the air,

And when the night came down upon the bogland
  With all-enveloping wings
The coal-black turf-stacks rose against the darkness
  Like the tombs of nameless kings.

IV

Galway

O the crossbones of Galway,
The hollow grey houses,
The rubbish and sewage,
The grass-grown pier,
And the dredger grumbling
All night in the harbour:
The war came down on us here.

Salmon in the Corrib
Gently swaying
And the water combed out
Over the weir
And a hundred swans
Dreaming on the harbour:
The war came down on us here.

The night was gay
With the moon and the Pleiads

But Mars was angry
On the hills of Clare
And September dawned
Upon willows and ruins:
The war came down on us here.

V

Clonmacnois

Eastward again, returning to our so-called posts,
We went out of our way to look at Clonmacnois—
A huddle of tombs and ruins of anonymous men
Above the Shannon dreaming in the quiet rain.

You millenarian dead, why should I arraign,
Being a part of it, the stupidity of men
Who cancel the voices of the heart with barbarous noise
And hide the barren facts of death in censored posts?

VI

Cushendun Again

The sky is a lather of stars,
Jupiter makes a stain upon the bay
But death is on the waters and no one
Can drive the war away.

The black horns of the headlands
Grip my gullet tight;

There is a dead calf on the beach
Like a black sack in the night.

The tide is out and the idle
Starlit wavelets play
But none of any of all the stars above me
Can drive the war away.

VII

Now It Has Happened

Why, now it has happened,
Should the clock go on striking to the firedogs
And why should the rooks be blown upon the evening
Like burnt paper in a chimney?

And why should the sea maintain its turbulence,
   Its elegance,
And draw a film of muslin down the sand
With each receding wave?
And why, now it has happened,
Should the atlas still be full of the maps of countries
We never shall see again?

And why, now it has happened,
And doom all night is lapping at the door,
Should I remember that I ever met you—
Once in another world?

                     [August–September, 1939]

MEETING POINT

Time was away and somewhere else,
There were two glasses and two chairs
And two people with the one pulse
(Somebody stopped the moving stairs):
Time was away and somewhere else,

And they were neither up nor down,
The stream's music did not stop
Flowing through heather, limpid brown,
Although they sat in a coffee shop
And they were neither up nor down.

The bell was silent in the air
Holding its inverted poise—
Between the clang and clang a flower,
A brazen calyx of no noise:
The bell was silent in the air.

The camels crossed the miles of sand
That stretched around the cups and plates;
The desert was their own, they planned
To portion out the stars and dates:
The camels crossed the miles of sand.

Time was away and somewhere else.
The waiter did not come, the clock
Forgot them and the radio waltz
Came out like water from a rock:
Time was away and somewhere else.

Her fingers flicked away the ash
That bloomed again in tropic trees:
Not caring if the markets crash
When they had forests such as these,
Her fingers flicked away the ash.

God or whatever means the Good
Be praised that time can stop like this,
That what the heart has understood
Can verify in the body's peace
God or whatever means the Good.

Time was away and she was here
And life no longer what it was,
The bell was silent in the air
And all the room a glow because
Time was away and she was here.

[April, 1939]

A TOAST

The slurred and drawled and crooning sounds,
The blurred and suave and sidling smells,
The webs of dew, the bells of buds,
The sun going down in crimson suds—
   This is on me and these are yours.

The bland and sculped and urgent beasts,
The here and there and nowhere birds,
The tongues of fire, the words of foam,
The curdling stars in the night's dome—
   This is on me and these are yours.

The face and grace and muscle of man,
The balance of his body and mind,
Who keeps a trump behind his brain
Till instinct flicks it out again—
    This is on me and these are yours.

The courage of eyes, the craft of hands,
The gay feet, the pulse of hope,
The will that flings a rope—though hard—
To catch the future off its guard—
    This is on me and these are yours.

The luck and pluck and plunge of blood,
The wealth and spilth and sport of breath,
And sleep come down like death above
The fever and the peace of love—
    This is on me and these are yours.

[May, 1939]

COMING FROM NOWHERE

Coming from nowhere
To nowhere Love
Makes him alone
Cut off from men
Like a grey bird
On a barren rock
Watching the seas
For what will rise.

What will rise?
The seas are rough;
Driftwood, weeds,
And glacial gleams.
Not here the goddess
Trod the foam,
The spring was never
Festal here.

A sombre numb
Prophetic cloud
Comes closer, closer
To his head,
Hunched on the rock
A pillared saint
With knees drawn up
And vacant eyes.

And on that rock
A thousand years
Of chafing salt
And cries of gulls
He sits and waits
Till time erodes
The walls of thought,
The thoughts of self

Until from nowhere
Again the sun
Unrolls a carpet;
Then he leaves
His rock and with

Deliberate feet
On golden water
Walks the world.

[February, 1940]

ORDER TO VIEW

It was a big house, bleak;
Grass on the drive;
We had been there before
But memory, weak in front of
A blistered door, could find
Nothing alive now;
The shrubbery dripped, a crypt
Of leafmould dreams; a tarnished
Arrow over an empty stable
Shifted a little in the almost wind,

And wishes were unable
To rise; on the garden wall
The pear trees had come loose
From rotten loops; one wish,
A rainbow bubble, rose,
Faltered, broke in the dull
Air— What was the use?
The bell-pull would not pull
And the whole place, one might
Have supposed, was deadly ill:
The world was closed,

And remained closed until
A sudden angry tree
Shook itself like a setter
Flouncing out of a pond
And beyond the sombre line
Of limes a cavalcade
Of clouds rose like a shout of
Defiance. Near at hand
Somewhere in a loose-box
A horse neighed
And all the curtains flew out of
The windows; the world was open.
                              [March, 1940]

NOVELETTES

I

The Old Story

The old story is true of charms fading;
He knew her first before her charm was mellow—
Slim; surprise in her eyes; like a woodland creature
Crept abroad who found the world amazing,

Who, afterwards maturing, yet was dainty,
Light on her feet and gentle with her fingers;
Put on a little flesh, became an easy
Spreadeagled beauty for Renaissance painters.

272

And then she went; he did not see her after
Until by the shore of a cold sea in winter
With years behind her and the waves behind her
Drubbing the memory up and down the pebbles.

Flotsam and wrack; the bag of old emotions;
Watch in the swirl her ten years back reflections—
White as a drowning hand, then gone for ever;
Here she stands who was twenty and is thirty.

The same but different and he found the difference
A surgeon's knife without an anaesthetic;
He had known of course that this happens
But had not guessed the pain of it or the panic,

And could not say 'My love,' could hardly
Say anything at all, no longer knowing
Whom he was talking to but watched the water
Massing for action on the cold horizon.

[Summer, 1939]

II

Suicide

He had fought for the wrong causes,
Had married the wrong wife,
Had invested rashly, had lost
His health and his reputation,
His fortune and his looks.

Who in his youth had gone
Walking on the crown of the road
Under delectable trees
And over irresponsible moors
To find the rainbow's end;

And was now, at forty-nine,
Living in a half timbered
Cottage with a pale
Mistress and some gardening
Books and a life of Napoleon.

When she left him he took
The shears and clipped the hedge
And then taking a shotgun
As if for duck went out
Walking on the crown of the road.

[Summer, 1939]

III

Les Sylphides

Life in a day: he took his girl to the ballet;
Being shortsighted himself could hardly see it—
  The white skirts in the grey
  Glade and the swell of the music
  Lifting the white sails.

Calyx upon calyx, canterbury bells in the breeze
The flowers on the left mirror to the flowers on the right
  And the naked arms above

The powdered faces moving
Like seaweed in a pool.

Now, he thought, we are floating—ageless, oarless—
Now there is no separation, from now on
   You will be wearing white
   Satin and a red sash
   Under the waltzing trees.

But the music stopped, the dancers took their curtain,
The river had come to a lock—a shuffle of programmes—
   And we cannot continue down
   Stream unless we are ready
   To enter the lock and drop.

So they were married—to be the more together—
And found they were never again so much together,
   Divided by the morning tea,
   By the evening paper,
   By children and tradesmen's bills.

Waking at times in the night she found assurance
In his regular breathing but wondered whether
   It was really worth it and where
   The river had flowed away
   And where were the white flowers.

[Summer, 1939]

IV

The Gardener

He was not able to read or write,
He did odd jobs on gentlemen's places
Cutting the hedge or hoeing the drive
With the smile of a saint,
With the pride of a feudal chief,
For he was not quite all there.

Crippled by rheumatism
By the time his hair was white,
He would reach the garden by twelve,
His legs in soiled puttees,
A clay pipe in his teeth,
A tiny flag in his cap,
A white cat behind him,
And his eyes a cornflower blue.
And between the clack of the shears
Or the honing of the scythe
Or the rattle of the rake on the gravel
He would talk to amuse the children,
He would talk to himself or the cat
Or the robin waiting for worms
Perched on the handle of the spade;
Would remember snatches of verse
From the elementary school
About a bee and a wasp
Or the cat by the barndoor spinning;
And would talk about himself for ever—
You would never find his like—

Always in the third person;
And would level his stick like a gun
(With a glint in his eye)
Saying 'Now I'm a Frenchman'—
He was not quite right in the head.

He believed in God—
The Good Fellow Up There—
And he used a simile of Homer
Watching the falling leaves,
And every year he waited for the Twelfth of July,
Cherishing his sash and his fife
For the carnival of banners and drums.
He was always claiming but never
Obtaining his old age pension,
For he did not know his age.
And his rheumatism at last
Kept him out of the processions.
And he came to work in the garden
Later and later in the day,
Leaving later at night;
In the damp dark of the night
At ten o'clock or later
You could hear him mowing the lawn,
The mower moving forward
And backward, forward and backward
For he mowed while standing still;
He was not quite up to the job.

But he took a pride in the job.
He kept a bowl of cold
Tea in the crotch of a tree,

Always enjoyed his food
And enjoyed honing the scythe
And making the potato drills
And putting the peasticks in;
And enjoyed the noise of the corncrake,
And the early hawthorn hedge
Peppered black and green,
And the cut grass dancing in the air—
Happy as the day was long.

Till his last sickness took him
And he could not leave his house
And his eyes lost their colour
And he sat by the little range
With a finch in a cage and a framed
Certificate of admission
Into the Orange Order,
And his speech began to wander
And memory ebbed
Leaving upon the shore
Odd shells and heads of wrack
And his soul went out on the ebbing
Tide in a trim boat
To find the Walls of Derry
Or the land of the Ever Young.

[Summer, 1939]

V

Christina

It all began so easy
With bricks upon the floor
Building motley houses
And knocking down your houses
And always building more.

The doll was called Christina,
Her underwear was lace,
She smiled while you dressed her
And when you then undressed her
She kept a smiling face.

Until the day she tumbled
And broke herself in two
And her legs and arms were hollow
And her yellow head was hollow
Behind her eyes of blue.

. . . .

He went to bed with a lady
Somewhere seen before,
He heard the name Christina
And suddenly saw Christina
Dead on the nursery floor.

[July, 1939]

VI

The Expert

The dilatory prophet, flicking the ash
On the Bokhara rug said 'Maybe yes;
When spring comes the markets will maybe crash,
Only the Unknown God can get us out of this mess.

Man is a political animal admittedly
But, politics being incalculable, I shall
With your permission pour myself another; I see
Nothing for it but to be animal.'

And putting the weight of his doctorates aside
Took three fingers of Scotch and a cube of ice
And thought that, could he announce that he had died,
And so was no longer an expert, it would be nice;

And drank till two, staring into the fire
Seeing half-naked girls, and then having collected
His courtesy and his hat, soft-pedalling desire
Went out to find the world as bad as he expected.

Drunk and alone among the indifferent lights
In stark unending streets of granite and glass
He ducked his head to avoid illusory stalactites
And fell, his brain ringing with the noise of brass

Captions; the groundswell of the pavement, steady
As fate, rose up and caught him, rolled him below
A truck—this ex-professor who had already
Outlived his job of being in the know.

[March, 1940]

VII

Provence

It is a decade now since he and she
Spent September in Provence: the vineyard
Was close about the house; mosquitoes and cicadas
Garrulous day and night; and by the sea
Thighs and shoulders tanning themselves and one
Gay old man in particular who never
Missed a day, a glutton for the sun,
But did not bathe. He and she with swimming
Every noon were wild for food; a Basque
Woman cooked on charcoal—aubergine with garlic,
And there were long green grapes exploding on the pal-
      ate
And smelling of eau de Cologne. They had nothing to ask
Except that it should go on. Watching the vintage—
A file of bullock carts and the muzzle of each
Animal munching purple—he suddenly said
'We must get married soon.' Down on the beach,
His wife and three of his three children dead,
An old man lay in the sun, perfectly happy.

[September, 1940]

VIII

The Preacher

He carried a ball of darkness with him, unrolled it
To find his way by in streets and rooms,
Every train or boat he took was Charon's ferry,
He never left the Catacombs;

281

He never smiled but spun his strands of black
Among the secular crowd who, when he tripped their
    feet,
Saw their own faces in the wet street, saw
Their hell beneath the street.

Among old iron, cinders, sizzling dumps,
A world castrated, amputated, trepanned,
He walked in the lost acres crying 'Repent
For the Kingdom of Death is at hand.'

He took the books of pagan art and read
Between the lines or worked them out to prove
Humanism a palimpsest and God's
Anger a more primal fact than love.

And in the city at night where drunken song
Climbed the air like tendrils of vine
He bared a knife and slashed the roots and laid
Another curse on Cain. The sign

Of the cross between his eyes, his mouth drawn down,
He passed the flower-sellers and all
The roses reeked of an abattoir, the gardenias
Became the décor of a funeral.

His hands were always clenched, an eagle
Riveted on a world of vice;
Going upstairs he built, block upon block,
An Aztec pyramid of sacrifice.

Going upstairs to die in a bare room
He tried to square his accounts; lying in bed

He summoned home his deeds, drew back
Sixty years' expended thread,

Pulled it in through the chink beneath the door,
Wrapped it around him, all
His faith and his despair a ball of black
And he himself at the centre of the ball.

[March, 1940]

THE GATES OF HORN

Through two gates
The visions come
That come to men—
True or untrue—;
The silent hinge
Again and again
Lets the jostling
Visions through,
The visions frantic to be born,
Those that are false
Through an ivory gate
But those that are true
Through the gates of horn.

The night she came
The clock had stopped
And the room no longer
Was the same,
I felt the cornice
Closing in

283

Like the petals of
A closing flower
And I cannot tell
How long she stayed,
I only know
That a sudden drum
Left me afraid
And the night was late
And that she had gone
As she had come—
Passing through the ivory gate.

There was no sound
In the afternoon
But the silence running
Round and round
Like a needle
On a gramophone
When the dog bristled
But did not bark
And I turned around
And there He was
And I said nothing
But in my mind
I cursed the day
That I was born,
But I said nothing—
Nothing because
He held the future in his hand,
He brought it through the gates of horn.

[October, 1939]

DÉBÂCLE

They had built it up—but not for this the lean
And divinatory years,
The red-eyed pioneers
Facing the dark and making the desert green.

Not for this the pale inventor's lamp
Alight till dawn, the hands
Weary with sifting sands,
The burst of nuggets on the miners' camp.

Vision and sinew made it of light and stone;
Not grateful nor enchanted
Their heirs took it for granted
Having a world—a world that was all their own.

At sundown now the windows had gone gold
For half an hour; a quick
Chill came off the brick
Walls and the flesh was suddenly old and cold.

Crumbling between the fingers, under the feet,
Crumbling behind the eyes,
Their world gives way and dies
And something twangs and breaks at the end of the
    street.

[September, 1940]

THREE THOUSAND MILES

Now he can hardly press
The heavy pedals of thought,
Tired of what he wants
And sick of what he ought,
He is content to watch
The window fill with snow
Making even the Future
Seem long ago.

Knowing that in Europe
All the streets are black
And that stars of blood
Star the almanac,
One half-hour's reprieve
Drowns him in the white
Physical or spiritual
Inhuman night.

[March, 1940]

DEATH OF AN ACTRESS

I see from the paper that Florrie Forde is dead—
Collapsed after singing to wounded soldiers,
At the age of sixty-five. The American notice
Says no doubt all that need be said

About this one-time chorus girl; whose rôle
For more than forty stifling years was giving
Sexual, sentimental, or comic entertainment,
A gaudy posy for the popular soul.

286

Plush and cigars: she waddled into the lights,
Old and huge and painted, in velvet and tiara,
Her voice gone but around her head an aura
Of all her vanilla-sweet forgotten vaudeville nights.

With an elephantine shimmy and a sugared wink
She threw a trellis of Dorothy Perkins roses
Around an audience come from slum and suburb
And weary of the tea-leaves in the sink;

Who found her songs a rainbow leading west
To the home they never had, to the chocolate Sunday
Of boy and girl, to cowslip time, to the never-
Ending weekend Islands of the Blest.

In the Isle of Man before the war before
The present one she made a ragtime favourite
Of 'Tipperary,' which became the swan-song
Of troop-ships on a darkened shore;

And during Munich sang her ancient quiz
Of *Where's Bill Bailey?* and the chorus answered,
Muddling through and glad to have no answer:
Where's Bill Bailey? How do *we* know where he is!

Now on a late and gangrened April day
In a military hospital Miss Florrie
Forde has made her positively last appearance
And taken her bow and gone correctly away.

Correctly. For she stood
For an older England, for children toddling

Hand in hand while the day was bright. Let the wren and
    robin
Gently with leaves cover the Babes in the Wood.

[May, 1940]

BAR-ROOM MATINS

Popcorn peanuts clams and gum:
We whose Kingdom has not come
Have mouths like men but still are dumb

Who only deal with Here and Now
As circumstances may allow:
The sponsored programme tells us how.

And yet the preachers tell the pews
What man misuses God can use:
Give us this day our daily news

That we may hear behind the brain
And through the sullen heat's migraine
The atavistic voice of Cain:

'Who entitled you to spy
From your easy heaven? Am I
My brother's keeper? Let him die.'

And God in words we soon forget
Answers through the radio set:
'The curse is on his forehead yet.'

Mass destruction, mass disease;
We thank thee, Lord, upon our knees
That we were born in times like these

When with doom tumbling from the sky
Each of us has an alibi
For doing nothing— Let him die.

Let him die, his death will be
A drop of water in the sea,
A journalist's commodity.

Pretzels crackers chips and beer:
Death is something that we fear
But it titillates the ear.

Anchovy almond ice and gin:
All shall die though none can win;
Let the Untergang begin—

Die the soldiers, die the Jews,
And all the breadless homeless queues.
Give us this day our daily news.

[July, 1940]

FLIGHT OF THE HEART

Heart, my heart, what will you do?
There are five lame dogs and one deaf-mute
All of them with demands on you.

I will build myself a copper tower
With four ways out and no way in
But mine the glory, mine the power.

And what if the tower should shake and fall
With three sharp taps and one big bang?
What would you do with yourself at all?

I would go in the cellar and drink the dark
With two quick sips and one long pull,
Drunk as a lord and gay as a lark.

But what when the cellar roof caves in
With one blue flash and nine old bones?
How, my heart, will you save your skin?

I will go back where I belong
With one foot first and both eyes blind,
I will go back where I belong
In the fore-being of mankind.

[October, 1940]

REFUGEES

With prune-dark eyes, thick lips, jostling each other
These, disinterred from Europe, throng the deck
To watch their hope heave up in steel and concrete
Powerful but delicate as a swan's neck,

Thinking, each of them, the worst is over
And we do not want any more to be prominent or rich,

Only to be ourselves, to be unmolested
And make ends meet—an ideal surely which

Here if anywhere is feasible. Their glances
Like wavering antennae feel
Around the sliding limber towers of Wall Street
And count the numbered docks and gingerly steal

Into the hinterland of their own future
Behind this excessive annunciation of towers,
Tracking their future selves through a continent of
       strangeness.
The liner moves to the magnet; the quay flowers

With faces of people's friends. But these are mostly
Friendless and all they look to meet
Is a secretary who holds his levée among ledgers,
Tells them to take a chair and wait . . .

And meanwhile the city will go on, regardless
Of any new arrival, trains like prayers
Radiating from stations haughty as cathedrals,
Tableaux of spring in milliners' windows, great affairs

Being endorsed on a vulcanite table, lines of washing
Feebly garish among grimy brick and dour
Iron fire-escapes; barrows of cement are rumbling
Up airy planks; a florist adds a flower

To a bouquet that is bound for somebody's beloved
Or for someone ill; in a sombre board-room great
Problems wait to be solved or shelved. The city
Goes on but you, you will probably find, must wait

Till something or other turns up. Something-or-Other
Becomes an expected angel from the sky
But do not trust the sky, the blue that looks so candid
Is non-committal, frigid as a harlot's eye.

Gangways—the handclasp of the land. The resurrected,
The brisk or resigned Lazaruses, who want
Another chance, go trooping ashore. But chances
Are dubious. Fate is stingy, recalcitrant

And officialdom greets them blankly as they fumble
Their foreign-looking baggage; they still feel
The movement of the ship while through their imagina-
    tion
Seen and unheard-of constellations wheel.

                                    [September, 1940]

JEHU

Peace on New England, on the shingled white houses,
    on golden
Rod and the red Turkey carpet spikes of sumach. The
    little
American flags are flapping in the graveyard. Continuous
    Chorus of grasshoppers. Fleece
Of quiet around the mind. Honeysuckle, phlox and
    smoke-bush,
Hollyhocks and nasturtium and corn on the cob. And
    the pine wood
    Smelling of outmoded peace.

A king sat over the gate looking to the desert. A spiral
Of dust came towards him, a special messenger asking
Anxiously 'Is it peace?' The heavy eyebrows lowered,
  He answered 'What have I
To do with peace?' and the messenger mopped the sweat
      and obedient
Took his place behind the king who still sat scanning
  Miles of desert and sky.

Negative prospect; sand in the lungs; blood in the sand;
      deceiving
Mirage of what were once ideals or even motives
And in this desert even a ghost can hardly
  Live—but in the long run what
Have I to do with life? He got up blandly, harnessed his
      horses
And furiously drove, his eyeballs burning and the
      chariot's
  Axles burning hot.

Someone sat in a window with a new coiffure, her raddled
Face, a Muse's possibly once but now a harlot's,
Smirked at the charioteer who, looking past her, signalled
  To the maids to throw her down
And they threw her down and the wheels went over her
      ribs and the carcase,
The one-time inspiration of artists, the toast of kings,
      was abandoned
  To the scavenger dogs of the town.

And now the sand blows over Kent and Wales where we
      may shortly

Learn the secret of the desert's purge, of the mad driving,
The cautery of the gangrened soul, though we are not
    certain
  Whether we shall stand beside
The charioteer, the surgeon, or shall be one with the
    pampered
Queen who tittered in the face of death, unable to
    imagine
  The meaning of the flood tide.

                           [August, 1940]

BALLADES

I

Ballade on an Old Theme

Where are now, in coign or crack,
The golden schedules that we made
Before the windows all went black,
Before the barren cannonade?
The magic word has been mislaid,
The page is missing from the book;
Having looked and looked we are afraid
That there is nowhere left to look.

Open the shutters front and back,
Look up and down the esplanade;
Bill and Silas, Neil and Jack,
Have vanished with the cavalcade
Of the befuddled and betrayed

294

Whose cherished time the demon took;
We wait in vain, their faces fade
And there is nowhere left to look.

Santa Claus has lost his sack;
Where are the toys we learnt to trade—
The dilettante bric-a-brac,
The ideologies of jade,
Where are the pompoms and the braid,
The trinkets of the private nook?
We have looked for them in sun and shade
And there is nowhere left to look.

Envoi

My friend, the horses that we played
Have failed to answer to the book;
We looked to see our fortunes made
But there is nowhere left to look.

[August, 1940]

II

Ballade for Mr. MacLeish

You say, who read, that we who write
Have failed to do our duty by
The blind and bogged who needed light,
The prisoners who needed sky,
The puzzled masses doomed to die,
The stunted youth that could not grow.
Yes, we failed and we know why:
You need not tell us what we know.

295

Easy to niggle and indict
Charges none of us deny:
We have not made the Negro white
Nor taught the wombat how to fly.
We neither caught the Future's eye
Nor yet preserved the *status quo*.
The world we found we left awry:
You need not tell us what we know.

We have not set the epoch right,
We would not if we had to lie;
Writers by trade we have tried to write
By evidence of mind and eye;
The day for that is perhaps gone by,
Truth is unfashionably slow
And shuns the opportune reply:
You need not tell us what we know.

Envoi

Gentry, you ask us to deny
The only right the arts bestow.
We know our failure to comply;
You need not tell us what we know.

[August, 1940]

III

Ballade in a Bad Temper

Gentlemen who boss the age—
Magistrate, magnate, editor,
Greasy priest and crooked sage,

Field Marshal and Prime Minister—
I have no liking to defer
To capitalist or bureaucrat;
As for your Social Register
You know what you can do with that!

And all you hacks who line the stage
To lick their boots and call them 'Sir,'
Your only habitat a cage,
Your only business to concur,
Excuse me if I must demur
At holding anybody's hat
(You say that it is *de rigueur?*)—
You know what you can do with that!

And you, the Moderates, who assuage
Their anger with a gentle purr
And lying low attempt to gauge
The way the weathercock will stir,
Your brains a mere barometer,
Who sold your birthright for a fat
Mess of pottage—I infer
You know what you can do with that!

Envoi

You too, my philanthropic sir,
Ready to skin the alley cat
If anyone would buy the fur—
You know what you can do with that!

[*August, 1940*]

IV

Ballade of Dirty Linen

Seeing that every dog, they say,
Whether snipy or undershot,
Cow-hocked or spavined, has his day,
It is natural that knave and sot
Who took their pickings from the pot
Should launch in print their Silhouettes,
Memoirs, Reflections, and what-not—
Dirty linen and regrets.

The generals who drew their pay
In the last war for God knows what—
Bats in the belfry, nuts in May—
Who did not seem to care a jot
How many of their men were shot
Wastefully at the Marne or Metz,
All that their disciples got
Was dirty linen and regrets.

Thug and welsher, all the array
Who let the enemy garrotte
The country, calling it o.k.,
Who held the helm and queered the yacht,
Who pulled their punches soon as not,
Their names may linger in Debrett's
Pages, the world will shroud the lot
In dirty linen and regrets.

Envoi

We too, unless we make a shot
To pay the universe our debts,
Can leave it nothing when we rot
But dirty linen and regrets.

[August, 1940]

V

Ballade for King Canute

England, granted, soon may be
Bankrupt; it is like as not.
King Canute forbade the sea
To flow beyond a certain spot
But there was something he forgot,
The waves came on, the court agreed
He had to shift his chair and trot
And cut his losses and proceed.

The old régime is out of key,
The furnace is no longer hot;
Dot your i and cross your t,
In either case the page will blot.
The nation has, for certain, shot
Her bolt unless she mend her creed
To match the life the times allot
And cut her losses and proceed.

Not to be compassed by decree,
Only a change of heart is what

Can give our life a *point d'appui*
And drain the pus and cure the rot.
The bibles of the past are not
Pertinent unless you read
Between the lines and choose the spot
To cut your losses and proceed.

Envoi

Citizens, our garden plot
Ravaged by blizzard, blight and weed,
Can bloom again if, broke or not,
We cut our losses and proceed.

[August, 1940]

O'CONNELL BRIDGE

Barrel-organ music:
The cold gold falls
From the lamps on the Liffey
In the chilly wind
And the crinkling river
Shivers the lights,
And night's companions
Are far to find.

Flotsam and jetsam
Our one-while loves
Blown like bubbles
In the trough of the sea,
Who are not the only
300

Lonely in bed:
I dread the darkness—
A mound on me.

Barrel-organ music—
A hackney cockney tune,
A rain of riches
In a lady's lap;
I give in answer
Not dance or spoken
Token but only
A coin in a cap.

[October, 1939]

THE DEATH-WISH

It being in this life forbidden to move
Too lightly, people, over-cautious, contrive
To save their lives by weighting them with dead
Habits, hopes, beliefs, anything not alive,
Till all this ballast of unreality sinks
The boat and all our thinking gurgles down
Into the deep sea that never thinks.

Which being so, it is not surprising that
Some in their impatience jump the rails,
Refusing to wait the communal failure, preferring
The way the madman or the meteor fails,
Deceiving themselves to think their death uncommon,
Avid to possess the unpossessable sea
As a man in spring desires to die in woman.

[May, 1940]

AUTOBIOGRAPHY

In my childhood trees were green
And there was plenty to be seen.

Come back early or never come.

My father made the walls resound,
He wore his collar the wrong way round.

Come back early or never come.

My mother wore a yellow dress;
Gently, gently, gentleness.

Come back early or never come.

When I was five the black dreams came;
Nothing after was quite the same.

Come back early or never come.

The dark was talking to the dead;
The lamp was dark beside my bed.

Come back early or never come.

When I woke they did not care;
Nobody, nobody was there.

Come back early or never come.

When my silent terror cried,
Nobody, nobody replied.

Come back early or never come.

I got up; the chilly sun
Saw me walk away alone.

Come back early or never come.
                                        [September, 1940]

CONVERSATION

Ordinary people are peculiar too:
Watch the vagrant in their eyes
Who sneaks away while they are talking with you
Into some black wood behind the skull,
Following un-, or other, realities,
Fishing for shadows in a pool.

But sometimes the vagrant comes the other way
Out of their eyes and into yours
Having mistaken you perhaps for yesterday
Or for to-morrow night, a wood in which
He may pick up among the pine-needles and burrs
The lost purse, the dropped stitch.

Vagrancy however is forbidden; ordinary men
Soon come back to normal, look you straight
In the eyes as if to say 'It will not happen again,'

Put up a barrage of common sense to baulk
Intimacy but by mistake interpolate
Swear-words like roses in their talk.

[March, 1940]

THE EAR

There are many sounds which are neither music nor
        voice,
There are many visitors in masks or in black glasses
Climbing the spiral staircase of the ear. The choice
Of callers is not ours. Behind the hedge
Of night they wait to pounce. A train passes,
The thin and audible end of a dark wedge.

We should like to lie alone in a deaf hollow
Cocoon of self where no person or thing would speak;
In fact we lie and listen as a man might follow
A will o' the wisp in an endless eyeless bog,
Follow the terrible drone of a cockchafer, or the bleak
Oracle of a barking dog.

[April, 1940]

THE SENSE OF SMELL

Smells: how many
Evocative poignant
Hypnotic pervading
Smells—the beanfield

304

(May's carousal);
The bonfire (autumn's
Mart of memory);
Turf-smoke for Ireland,
Wine for France;
Moss-rose, jasmine
For love—and violets;
Homesick rosemary;
Lavender; mint;
Buddleia (loud
With bees) and clover;
Trees in rain;
Tar for travel.

And the smells indoors:
Pantry and kitchen—
Chicken in casserole,
Baking bread,
Cheddar, cinnamon,
Herring and mackerel,
Coffee in the morning,
Oil and garlic.
Each of the rooms
A different blend—
Beeswax, hyacinth
And burning logs;
Leather and pipe-smoke;
Trunks and damp;
French fern soap
And bath powder;
Witch-hazel, talc,

Laundered linen;
Smells of domestic
Peace, routine.

Social smells:
Office and warehouse,
Factory and train;
Urine and soot
And Diesel oil.
Smell of a church—
Hassocks and prayerbooks,
Varnished pews
And brass polish,
Odour of sanctity,
Gas and mortar.
Smells of hotels—
Cigars and soap.
Smells of the cinema
Real and fancied—
The fancy sweet
With the spice of China,
Attar of summer
And Arabian wafts,
Plush and cheap
Scent and stale
Smoke the reality.
Smell of the work-gang:
Coke in a brazier,
Sweat, corduroy,
Shirts they sleep in,
Beer and shag,
Cement, tarpaulin.

Smells of the rich:
Blend of indulgence—
Turkish tobacco,
Punch and gin,
Perfumed women
And men's barbers,
Eau de Cologne
And Harris tweed.
Smells of shops:
Heterogeneous,
Stippled and dappled,
Jazz and jigsaw,
Clamour of groceries,
Candles, fish,
Meths and turps,
Rolls of carpets.
Smell of the roads:
Of hedge and moor,
Gasoline, rubber,
Asphalt, carbon,
Flax and pinewood,
Tar and wind.
Smell of the ports:
Bales and pitch,
Crates of oranges,
Anthracite,
Terra Incognita,
Foreign flesh.
Smells of farms:
Goats and cowdung,
Hay and gaiters,
Udder and crupper,

A wet dog lying
On the parlour floor,
Hanging halters,
Mash and bran.

And whatever the place
At whatever time
The smells we cannot
Name but known
Smells and some
Unknown but ours.

And how many others
Linked for different
People with different
Times and people,
Historic, exotic,
Chains and fountains;
Smells that become
Picture and music,
Prayer and communion,
Challenge and anthem,
Ghost and angel,
Dissolving the present
Moment and changing
Season and tone
Back to a vanished
April, an ended
Voyage, a picnic
On grass that now
Is pavement; sweeping
Us back to islands

That are off the map,
To forbidden bedrooms
In demolished houses,
Homes we left
Or ports we touched at,
Back to a walled
Garden or a wood,
To a street or a field,
To nursery or bistro,
To unusual or usual
Days, to forgotten
Slang, to abandoned
Habits, to men
And women and children.

Smells—how many
Tricky, deceiving
Luminous Will
O' the Wisps, Aladdin's
Lamps that are lost
When hardly lit,
Bricked-up arches
Suddenly open
Revealing roads
Or woodland alleys
But bricked-up arches
Before we enter.
How many delights?
How many adieus?

[September, 1940]

EVENING IN CONNECTICUT

Equipoise: becalmed
Trees, a dome of kindness;
Only the scissory noise of the grasshoppers;
Only the shadows longer and longer.

The lawn a raft
In a sea of singing insects,
Sea without waves or mines or premonitions:
Life on a china cup.

But turning. The trees turn
Soon to brocaded autumn.
Fall. The fall of dynasties; the emergence
Of sleeping kings from caves—

Beard over the breastplate,
Eyes not yet in focus, red
Hair on the back of the hands, unreal
Heraldic axe in the hands.

Unreal but still can strike.
And in defence we cannot call on the evening
Or the seeming-friendly woods—
Nature is not to be trusted,

Nature whose falls of snow,
Falling softer than catkins,
Bury the lost and over their grave a distant
Smile spreads in the sun.

Not to be trusted, no,
Deaf at the best; she is only
And always herself, Nature is only herself,
Only the shadows longer and longer.

[September, 1940]

OCTETS

I

Interregnum

Twenty years forgetting,
Twenty years turning the Nelson eye,
Our wings heavy with the pollen
Of flowers about to die

We said 'Make merry in the sunshine,
At least we are alive,'
But now the sun has set behind the hangar,
There is no honey in the hive.

II

Barcelona in Wartime

In the Paralelo a one-legged
Man sat on the ground,
His one leg out before him,
Smiling. A sudden sound

311

Of crazy laughter shivered
The sunlight; overhead
A parrot in a window of aspidistras
Was laughing like the dead.

III

November Afternoon

Autumn and the war outside
And a shrinking candle in the mind
And the milky Michaelmas daisies
Cowering in the wind.

I look into the dim
Mirror in the hall and see
A faded portrait, a drowned
Face looking back at me.

IV

Radio

Science has given me a knob;
I turn it round and hear
Voices from every country
Wrangling for my ear;

Bubbles upon bubbles
Out of the unknown,
I count them and remember
Men can drown.

V

Shopping

Below the sealskin coat
The high-heeled ankles give;
Someone is suffering from
A dead prerogative,

Trailing from shop to shop,
Pondering what to buy,
Ignoring like Belshazzar
The writing on the sky.

VI

Business Men

The two men talking business
So easily in the train
Project themselves upon me
Just as the windowpane

Reflects their faces, and I
Find myself in a trance
To hear two strangers talking
The same language for once.

VII

Night Club

After the legshows and the brandies
And all the pick-me-ups for tired
Men there is a feeling
Something more is required.

The lights go down and eyes
Look up across the room;
Salome comes in, bearing
The head of God knows whom.

VIII

The Lecher

He lies alone and the tepid
Memories creep round him,
The same coral sea
That often drowned him.

Somewhere at the bottom
Of the last lagoon
Is the first girl he met
And all her year is June.

314

IX

Prospect

With her too delicate sensitivity
And her clumsy hands
She stood on a hill with a wide prospect
Looking across the dangerous lands

Looking for the place she wants—
Wants too much—
That her soul knows but her hands
Have lost the sense of touch.

X

Didymus

Refusing to fall in love with God, he gave
Himself to the love of created things,
Accepting only what he could see, a river
Full of the shadows of swallows' wings

That dipped and skimmed the water; he would not
Ask where the water ran or why.
When he died a swallow seemed to plunge
Into the reflected, the wrong, sky.

[October–November, 1939]

PLURALITY

It is patent to the eye that cannot face the sun
The smug philosophers lie who say the world is one,
World is other and other, world is here and there,
Parmenides would smother life for lack of air
Precluding birth and death; his crystal never breaks—
No movement and no breath, no progress nor mistakes,
Nothing begins or ends, no one loves or fights,
All your foes are friends and all your days are nights
And all the roads lead round and are not roads at all
And the soul is muscle-bound, the world a wooden ball.
The modern monist too castrates, negates our lives
And nothing that we do, make or become survives,
His terror of confusion freezes the flowing stream
Into mere illusion, his craving for supreme
Completeness means he chokes each orifice with tight
Plaster as he evokes a dead ideal of white
All-white Universal, refusing to allow
Division or dispersal—Eternity is now
And Now is therefore numb, a fact he does not see
Postulating a dumb static identity
Of Essence and Existence which could not fuse without
Banishing to a distance belief along with doubt,
Action along with error, growth along with gaps;
If man is a mere mirror of God, the gods collapse.
No, the formula fails that fails to make it clear
That only change prevails, that the seasons make the
      year,
That a thing, a beast, a man is what it is because
It is something that began and is not what it was,
Yet is itself throughout, fluttering and unfurled,

316

Not to be cancelled out, not to be merged in world,
Its entity a denial of all that is not it,
Its every move a trial through chaos and the Pit,
An absolute and so defiant of the One
Absolute, the row of noughts where time is done,
Where nothing goes or comes and Is is one with Ought
And all the possible sums alike resolve to nought.
World is not like that, world is full of blind
Gulfs across the flat, jags against the mind,
Swollen or diminished according to the dice,
Foaming, never finished, never the same twice.
You talk of Ultimate Value, universal Form—
Visions, let me tell you, that ride upon the storm
And must be made and sought but cannot be maintained,
Lost as soon as caught, always to be regained,
Mainspring of our striving towards perfection, yet
Would not be worth achieving if the world were set
Fair, if error and choice did not exist, if dumb
World should find its voice for good and God become
Incarnate once for all. No, perfection means
Something but must fall unless there intervenes
Between that meaning and the matter it should fill
Time's revolving hand that never can be still.
Which being so and life a ferment, you and I
Can only live by strife in that the living die,
And, if we use the word Eternal, stake a claim
Only to what a bird can find within the frame
Of momentary flight (the value will persist
But as event the night sweeps it away in mist).
Man is man because he might have been a beast
And is not what he was and feels himself increased,
Man is man in as much as he is not god and yet

Hankers to see and touch the pantheon and forget
The means within the end and man is truly man
In that he would transcend and flout the human span:
A species become rich by seeing things as wrong
And patching them, to which I am proud that I belong.
Man is surely mad with discontent, he is hurled
By lovely hopes or bad dreams against the world,
Raising a frail scaffold in never-ending flux,
Stubbornly when baffled fumbling the stubborn crux
And so he must continue, raiding the abyss
With aching bone and sinew, conscious of things amiss,
Conscious of guilt and vast inadequacy and the sick
Ego and the broken past and the clock that goes too
        quick,
Conscious of waste of labour, conscious of spite and hate,
Of dissension with his neighbour, of beggars at the gate,
But conscious also of love and the joy of things and the
        power
Of going beyond and above the limit of the lagging
        hour,
Conscious of sunlight, conscious of death's inveigling
        touch,
Not completely conscious but partly—and that is much.
                                        [August, 1940]

THE UNDENIABLE FACT

In the beginning and in the end the only decent
Definition is tautology: man is man,
Woman woman, and tree tree, and world world,
Slippery, self-contained; catch as catch can.

Which when caught between the beginning and end
Turn other than themselves, their entities unfurled,
Flapping and overlapping—a tree becomes
A talking tower, and a woman becomes world.

Catch them in nets, but either the thread is thin
Or the mesh too big or, thirdly, the fish die
And man from false communion dwindles back
Into a mere man under a mere sky.

But dream was dream and love was love and what
Happened happened—even if the judge said
It should have been otherwise—and glitter glitters
And I am I although the dead are dead.

[March, 1940]

PERDITA

The glamour of the end attic, the smell of old
Leather trunks—Perdita, where have you been
Hiding all these years? Somewhere or other a green
Flag is waving under an iron vault
And a brass bell is the herald of green country
And the wind is in the wires and the broom is gold.

Perdita, what became of all the things
We said that we should do? The cobwebs cover
The labels of Tyrol. The time is over-
Due and in some metropolitan station
Among the clank of cans and the roistering files
Of steam the caterpillars wait for wings.

[March, 1940]

THE DOWSER

An inkling only, whisper in the bones
Of strange weather on the way,
Twitch of the eyelid, shadow of a passing bird.
It is coming some time soon.

What? or who? An inkling only,
Adumbration of unknown glory
Drew to the feet of Saint Francis where the waves
Broke, an army of fish.

Humming wires; feel of a lost limb
Cut off in another life;
Trance on the tripod; effulgence
Of headlights beyond the rise in the road.

And the hazel rod bent, dipping, contorting,
Snake from sleep; they were right
Who remembered some old fellow
(Dead long ago) who remembered the well.

'Dig,' he said, 'dig,'
Holding the lantern, the rod bent double,
And we dug respecting his knowledge,
Not waiting for morning, keenly

Dug: the clay was heavy
Two hours heavy before
The clink of a spade revealed
What or whom? We expected a well—

A well? A mistake somewhere . . .
More of a tomb. . . . Anyway we backed away
From the geyser suddenly of light that erupted, sprayed
Rocketing over the sky azaleas and gladioli.

[September, 1940]

THE RETURN

All the lost interpretations,
All the unconsummated consummations,
All the birds that flew and left the big sky empty
Come back throwing shadows on our patience.

Bethlehem is desolate and the stables
Cobwebbed, mute; below each Tower of Babel's
Sentrydom of night, inside the bleak
Glass of cafés chairs are piled on tables.

Notwithstanding which, notwithstanding
The hospital—the icicles round the landing—
Expecting Birth, we know that it will come
Sooner or later, banding

Together the good daemons, the defiance
And lolloping vulcanite of sea-lions,
The harlequinade of water through a sluice,
Tigers in the air, and in the teeth of science

The acclamation of earth's returning daughter,
Jonquils out of hell, and after
Hell the imperative of joy, the dancing
Fusillade of sunlight on the water.

[February, 1940]

CRADLE SONG

For Eleanor

Sleep, my darling, sleep:
   The pity of it all
Is all we compass if
   We watch disaster fall;
Put off your twenty-odd
   Encumbered years and creep
Into the only heaven,
   The robbers' cave of sleep.

The wild grass will whisper,
   Lights of passing cars
Will streak across your dreams
   And fumble at the stars;
Life will tap the window
   Only too soon again,
Life will have her answer—
   Do not ask her when.

When the winsome bubble
   Shivers, when the bough
Breaks, will be the moment
   But not here or now.
Sleep and, asleep, forget
   The watchers on the wall
Awake all night who know
   The pity of it all.

[October, 1940]

INDEX OF FIRST LINES